Love it,
don't
Label it!

God dips from a thread
   And is born once more in me.
The circle's so limiting
   My soul spirals free.
Will you come to know me?
   The circle rounds again.
I weep for the souls that pass
   Content to track where they've been.

A Practical Guide For Using
Spiritual Principles In Everyday Life

Carlin Diamond

Fifth Wave Press
San Rafael, California

Illustrated by Marybeth L. Rapisardo

Editor: Kimberley M. Peterson
Cover design: Kathleen Vande Kieft
Cover photography: Chris Thomerson
Text design: Merrill Peterson
Production Coordination: Matrix Productions
Composition: G & S Typesetters, Inc.

Library of Congress Cataloging in Publication Data

Diamond, Carlin J. (Carlin Jo), 1938–
    Love it, don't label it.

    1. Spiritual life.   2. Diamond, Carlin J. (Carlin Jo), 1938–   . I. Title.
BL624.D53   1986   158'.1   85-80399
ISBN 0-911761-03-9

9 8 7 6 5 4 3 2 1

Dedicated With Devotion
To Children

To these patient child-teachers who have chosen
to intimately share in my life. I feel blessed with the
valuable lessons they are sharing with me.

Dane who is teaching Mom Love
Evan who is teaching Mama Joy
Aaron who is teaching Mommy Trust
Angela who is teaching Carlin Acceptance
Jemal who is teaching Carlin Gratitude
Cara who is teaching Carlin to live
in the Present Moment

To the Child within us all

The Playful and Creative Child
who flowers with encouragement
The Abused and Neglected Child
who can be loved and released

Contents

Preface

My enlightenment process has had a simple and basic core: as long as I felt I had to have something or someone, I manipulated and tried to control things in order to get what I thought I wanted. It turns out that I really wanted freedom from this conditional, bargaining way of being in this world. During the enlightenment process I had to let go of all my needs, judgments, criticisms, must-haves, and addictions. But the most difficult part has been sustaining my devotion to the practices I felt were beneficial to my growth.

Though it seemed quite easy at first, I soon broke through the surface and delved into my "less conscious" areas of motivation. Here I found fears with no logic or reason, no apparent cause and effect; they did not readily submit to my customary scrutiny and analysis so they were not easily understood. I was now dealing with feelings: anger and resentment, old wells of stagnant misery that seemed to defy my usual process of recognition and release. I was full of unknown fears that were standing in the way of my attempts to love unconditionally and to experience the peace of mind that I so desired.

I saw reflected in my behavior not a world moving toward enlightenment but a world of escape through work, drugs, alcohol, and hard play. Rather than cultivating spiritual growth, people seemed to be leaving their holy practices to experts, giving their parental teaching responsibilities away, and teaching only by talk, not by action and example. I also saw the starry-eyed spiritual leaders who had only moved their ego needs from the work-a-day world into the spiritual realm, still grabbing for power and things of the world to decorate and embellish an image that would impress others.

I saw and I judged and then I let go of the judgments. There was truth in everything, and my task was to find my own truth and help others find theirs. I have been developing my process for over fifteen years with the help of many wonderful people who shared my questions and concerns about spirituality. Together we have talked and explored and found our individual paths, forging tools that are ready when our peace of mind or unconditional love falters. Through practice I no longer act as if spirituality is a separate aspect of life, to be practiced one day a week. It is an integral part of every action I take and of every thought I conceive.

Love It, Don't Label It traces the process of my spiritual evolution. It grew out of "Scenario for a Play" (see Chapter Three, "Belief Systems"); a piece that was inspired by my desire to find humor in the inconsistencies of our belief systems. After sharing "Scenario" with friends, I was encouraged to continue writing to communicate to others the simplicity I have discovered in my own process of spiritual evolution. It has been a magnificent task for me.

This book aims to demystify the process of enlightenment, to bring it out of the mystical/magical realm where it is considered too esoteric for direct interpretation, and into the everyday world. It will show you how to bring this process alive in your life.

I have five main goals in mind in writing this book:

1. To demonstrate the separation that results from labeling and defending ourselves and how this keeps us stuck in addictive modes of behavior.

2. To examine our less-conscious belief systems as well as our conscious ones.

3. To help us feel comfortable with our less-conscious areas of awareness. These areas are a natural part of us and ready for exploration.

4. To approach spiritual evolution as a constant process of letting go, of surrendering the parts of us that are so fearful they block access to our larger awareness.

5. To create, prioritize, and develop new habits that can begin to serve us today. Included are ways of maintaining and supporting a more productive perception of the world.

My journey is offered with love and compassion and caring for us all on our honorable paths to understanding and gaining a wider perspective. If I take myself a little too seriously at times, please forgive me; I only wish for you the joy and peace of mind that are my present constant companions—friends I have made through the practices I present to you here.

I encourage you to value yourself enough to start some of the suggested practices and to value your family, friends, and world enough to set an example for them.

Please consider reading the epilogue for a further summary of the book. As there really is no beginning and no end, perhaps you will find some focus for your reading there.

Note

I have found the gender-related personal pro-
nouns—"he," "she," or the neutered form, "it"—
to be a shortcoming of our language. I did a lot
of rewriting in an attempt to avoid, without too
much awkwardness, using "he" or "she" in reference to a human experience equally available to
us all. As a woman, I have longed to read a book
without having to automatically translate "he" to
"she" or philosophically address the male aspect
of myself to justify the chosen masculine pronoun.

"I" and "we" even feel confining as I grow toward feeling less boundaries between us in the
human experience we are creating and sharing. I
pondered as I wrote: does the English language
reflect separation or does it perpetuate it?

Introduction

I will take you in a moment on a journey into my less conscious levels of awareness, to experience, as much as possible, a level of consciousness that combines forgotten experiences and impressions with information that has come to me from unknown places. I have caught fleeting glimpses of this mixture throughout my life. Often, when my conscious mind can accept knowledge from my less conscious resources, I have a dream, a vision, or a meditation experience that presents the information clearly. The synthesis that occurs at this time is helpful in clarifying patterns of behavior, or in revealing sequences of events in my life that teach me something.

I have always known that my birth was a difficult one, so I have left it unexplored all my life. When rebirthing became the latest "new age" tool I decided it was one I could do nicely without. While Past-life Regressions took me close, although not too close, to my birth time, this was an area I instinctively knew was off-limits for my psyche.

However, in the course of writing this book, I had a profound remembrance of my birth experience. I awoke one morning from a dream that I knew would be overwhelmingly significant in my life. I immediately wrote down every detail and feeling, not even wanting to move lest I forget the tiniest fragments. Every impression seemed urgent and alive with importance.

My husband was available as a helpful listener as I sorted out the images enough to share them with him. The tears flowed and my voice choked with emotion as my dream images unfolded in great detail. As I talked, this magnificent dream was transformed into a passionate vision. Here is the dream:

> A friend and I left a group of people and skipped off to climb a hill. Part way up the hill we followed some others into a cave-like tunnel entrance. I went feet first, sliding down through a soft tube that narrowed as I went. Others before me were getting through so I didn't panic, but it *was* feeling awfully close. I could only move with an undulating motion of my body. . . .

I came out of the dream before I had completed my transit through the tube. Upon awakening, I felt a kink in time, as if time had stood still. I recognized this feeling, having experienced it many times while meditating, and I was grateful I had time to explore this moment without interruption.

As the vision unfolded, I didn't even want to breathe loudly for fear of disturbing the experience. It was as if all the usual life rhythms had been put on hold while I explored the moment in slow motion detail. Often, in the busy-ness of our lives, the opportunity to stay with these moments is lost.

As I shared the vision with my husband, I was overwhelmed by deep feelings and inarticulate sobs of grief—

emotions from that deep, aching space I only visit when I feel really safe. This place houses my deepest fears— maybe people aren't really good inside, there is no rhyme or reason to life, no one would notice if I died, greed and grasping are all there is—fears that I must feel very strong, confident, and safe to face.

One message the vision conveyed was: *my resistance won't block the way to getting my work done on earth!* This message relieved me of a heavy burden I had un-knowingly carried for a long time. I discovered in that mo-ment I had been feeling guilty for analyzing and resisting my intuition. This message freed me by telling me that although I may sometimes do it the hard way, that is my choice; I need never doubt that my work *is* being accom-plished. This was a tremendous relief. I hadn't realized how heavy the burden was until I recognized I'd been carrying it and set it down.

The Prologue that follows describes the vision that came from the dream, the emotions that accompanied the dream, and the special moment of feeling that told me I was participating in another level of consciousness. The dream recollection and vision lasted only a few minutes; it took a couple of hours to write it all down, but it took days to "translate" it into a form I could share with you, the reader. Translation of experiences from these realms is a difficult and fascinating process to undertake.

The vision I share now starts with a soul's intention, moves to the reality of birth into a body and the memory loss which accompanies birth, and into the process of a person "evolving" in this life. In this vision, hundreds of fragments of past experience flow into a pattern that ex-plains a lifetime of fear and resistance, and clarifies my lifelong search for spiritual connection and my deep de-sire for knowledge of order in the universe. This vision, and others I have experienced like it, have helped me to gain a deep perspective on life and provide me with a view-point from which I feel able to make appropriate choices about my spiritual development.

I believe that a vast area of awareness is not always accessible to the conscious mind. In this vast, partially explored area lies our total memory, encompassing centuries of evolutionary development to the beginning of this life. Here we will find the power of healing; dream playgrounds; visions; prophecies; a connection with everyone and everything, alive and dead; and much more. These areas connect to the conscious mind when we are ready, capable of understanding their depth. The method of connection will suit the personality and the readiness of each individual. Remember: *nothing and no one can take you into areas that you are not, on some level, ready to explore.* Nothing will come to your conscious awareness that you don't have the resources to handle.

Often, much of what comes to the conscious mind from these other levels of awareness is dismissed as irrelevant, needing too much translation. However, with patience and introspection, we can soon learn to decipher such experiences and learn all that we care to know about anything we focus on in our inner or outer world. For me, meditation is the most direct and independent means by which to enter visionary states. Meditation is a tool which we can use to deal effectively with all the changes in our lives. It leads us directly into taking responsibility for our intentions and actions. I see *spirituality as accepting responsibility for creating our reality.*

As a good swimming instructor would do, I have given you a little preparation for the experience to come; now it is time to get into the water. So, without any further attempt at clarification at this time, please jump into the pool with me. After the first dip we will learn some more tips about swimming, and about how to enjoy the water.

Love it, don't Label it!

Prologue

The tremendous joy of being born into a body once more . . . taking the message of joy and peace and healing to the earth. . . . Being in a body brings back such wonderful memories. This time I choose an attractive form that will draw many people to the peace of God through me. I have a few physical frailties . . . having spent so much time away, I'll need some "reminders to stay in the body on the earth." My work is simple: bringing peace of mind and love into the practical earth realm so that it can be understood by all and put into everyday use. It will be such a joy teaching people to put peace into their relationships and their world once more. I choose a gentle part of the world to be born into, to grow in love with a large family so I might learn all about many different relationships.

I pick a beautiful father and mother and find myself growing in her womb. My body is growing terribly fast; it is cozy and warm for awhile. Then

the first twinge of pain starts. At first it is like a memory
. . . remembering the weight of the body . . . but this is
pain . . . I am remembering the pain. I had forgotten the
pain of the body. Can I deal with it? My body isn't hurting,
my mother is hurting and I feel her pain . . . sharing the
pain . . . the pain becomes my own discomfort . . . I feel
fear, awful fear pouring through my veins . . . I hear fear
. . . feel fear . . . taste fear . . . I feel my first closing to the
sounds of pain . . . I feel fear, awful fear pouring through
my veins . . . I am absorbed in the pain . . . my whole consciousness becomes pain . . . I had forgotten the pain of
being alone . . . this is it . . . pain . . .

I want to go back . . . I'm almost forgetting already to
where . . . I just want to go back . . . I can't . . . my body is
getting enormous . . . and the shouting and the pain . . . I
change my mind, I can't do this . . . I am not ready . . . Oh
please let me go back . . . please . . . I'll come another time
. . . I can't do it. God is saying something to me . . . I can't
hear . . . wait, I can't hear. Water rushes by. . . the walls
are squeezing me. . . .

I am on my way out . . . no . . . no . . . no . . . wait, I've
got to hear . . . the contractions ease . . . my mother and I
slip into and out of sleep many times . . . contractions
come and go . . . the tightness around my head is unbearable . . . I sleep in pain . . . then jar into consciousness with more squeezing . . . I don't want to go . . . *no*, I
am screaming with resistance to leaving . . . the hurt here
is so intense . . . NO! NO! NO! . . . and the birth is inter-
minable. My mother is suffering . . . I want to die and go
back . . . it is no good . . . I've come too soon . . . I can't do
it . . . I am losing touch with my purpose by being born
. . . I'm doing it all wrong . . . and the tube is too small
and my head and neck and shoulders hurt and it is so
slow . . . no one knows my pain . . . my mother's pain . . .
I'm sorry . . . I'm sorry . . . I'm doing it all wrong . . . it's
the wrong time . . . I'm here too soon . . . hours and hours
turn into days . . . and one, two, three days go by in and
out of consciousness . . . stuck in resistance and indeci-

sion and the paralysis of fear . . . I'm sorry . . . I'm sorry
. . . If I'm born I lose touch with God . . . no . . . let me go
back . . . please!!!! Help me . . . Mother's pushing . . .
someone is pulling on my head . . . I am resisting . . . they
are taking me away from God . . . NO! NO! Oh the pain
. . . it is burning into me . . . I can't remember anything
. . . Where is God? God is gone . . . I am ALONE!!! no one
knows me here! . . . I can't remember what I am to do . . .
what is it? Is anyone here to help me? . . . don't leave me
. . . the pain . . . I look out into this world. I AM ALONE
WITH PAIN . . . EVERYONE HAS THEIR OWN PAIN . . .
WE STAND SIDE BY SIDE BUT DON'T JOIN . . . WE ARE
ABSORBED WITH RELENTLESS PAIN . . . I AM NOT
ALONE IN EXPERIENCING IT . . . BUT I AM ALONE . . .
WALLS OF MISERY DIVIDE US . . . AND I LOOK AROUND
ME AND ONLY SEE THE WALLS . . . LET ME COME
HOME GOD, I CAN'T DO THIS . . . THE JOB IS TOO BIG
FOR ME.

And I breathe . . . air singes my lungs and I dry up and
my skin feels no moisture and the dryness makes me feel
like I will crack . . . and everything aches . . . and they
bathe me and wrap me and say I am fine . . . I'm not fine
. . . I hurt . . . no one understands . . . I hurt so much . . .
the noises . . . everything crashes . . . metal clanks . . .
bright lights too bright . . . cloth too white . . . fiber too
harsh . . . mattress too hard. I want skin and warmth and
nursing . . . skin and warmth . . . metal too cold . . .
touches too brusque . . . I cry and cry and ache and am
so lonely . . . so alone . . . I don't like this body . . . it hurts
. . . I am helpless . . . scared . . . I recoil and pull in tighter
and tighter . . . curling in . . . I get small and smaller,
maybe small enough to go back . . . I just want to nurse
and they take me away . . . I cry to be back with the skin
and warmth . . . they give me a bottle and I cry . . . No, the
skin . . . more skin and I tell them and no one hears me
. . . I am so frightened . . . how can I be understood in
this world . . . no one listens . . . what I need I can't seem
to get . . . I'll die . . . and a fear of death comes and the

pain of fire consumes me . . . burning my memory like a beam of scorching, intense light . . . and I forget about what was before.

I am alone . . . I have just the present moment . . . I am afraid to move . . . there is no past memory . . . just lonely feeling . . . and survival with this body . . . contracted . . . pulled in tight . . . ready to spring out and attack . . . aha! that is why I am so contracted . . . for defense . . . like a rattlesnake coiled up to strike . . . ready before they get me . . . a survival tool for this primitive new life . . . I am now in this body . . . defensive and ready!

Outside, the world hears my crying grow quieter. Inside, I rage and fester in the darkness of my fears. Outside, my nice-little-girl image survives. Inside, the angry woman grows, matures, becomes. The fear of being on the wrong planet lingers. There is no one to communicate with . . . my language doesn't seem to fit . . . I do all the right things so no one yells at me . . . but no one really *hears* me.

1

Sacred Inner Feelings

For as long as I can remember I have felt like an observer, as if I was peeking out at the world from deep down within myself through a periscope. I also remember being in both physical and emotional pain for the greater part of my life. No one knew the pain I felt as a child because I hid it so well. I suspected others were feeling as I did, although I never seemed to connect with any of them. At times I thought I was crazy; this gave me all the more reason for keeping my pain to myself.

By age seven, I had tired of constant illness so I decided to make a wish. I looked up to the sky thinking that if I could have one request it would be for health. This memory is so strong that even now I can still clearly see where I was at the time: the water meter plate set in concrete, surrounded by grass near the sidewalk; I was walking to the dentist. (I had this strong sense of my own history from an early age. I clearly remember making

mental notes at seemingly insignificant times to record every tree leaf, smell, sound, and thought for future reference. It seemed important to record the less significant events as well as the more dramatic ones.) Somehow my request was answered, because after this my health improved for awhile.

At the age of nine I began to have migraine headaches. (Looking back on these headaches now, it occurs to me they may have been reminders of my birth pain.) It was also at this age that I began to feel drawn to organized religion. I attended a variety of churches, usually by myself or with a girlfriend; sometimes with my aunts. I did not like Sunday School at all. The teachers talked down to us, gave us stars to control our behavior, gave us already-drawn pictures to color in, fed us cookies, and separated us by age. I enjoyed children of other ages, both younger and older, and resented the fact that I couldn't be with them. However, the worst part of Sunday School was the condescending adult talk we children had to endure. Like a nice little girl, I politely quit going rather than tell them that their attitude toward me was repugnant. (Yes, that *was* the word I used then.) I wanted to be in with the adults in the big room with all of the candles and robes and statues and music.

When I was ten I asked God if there was any way to remain soft and caring without becoming hard. I had realized that putting up my defenses against emotional hurt could, itself, prove painful. As I made this request, I also made a silent vow to myself that I wouldn't become too hard and unfeeling, no matter what happened to me. It was frightening to make that vow—I wasn't at all sure if I could keep it and I took my vows very seriously. Nevertheless, at times I did close down on my soft and vulnerable place. In many cases, I recoiled and withdrew so skillfully that others weren't even aware of my wound. Something in me didn't want others to know I had not taken steps to protect myself. I felt it was bad not to have defended my sacred place more carefully; I felt I should be tougher and not let my feelings show.

This attitude was reinforced by experiences such as the following: Sarah Lee Van Deusen was a school friend. We were always involved in a subtle, unacknowledged, feminine competition as rivals for the title of "best" or "nicest" in class, or "teacher's pet," or the "smartest." She won hands down in the "long blonde ringlets" department. We maintained a strained but working friendship until I won the third-grade spelling bee and its coveted prize: an Uncle Remus Storybook. I was overjoyed by the victory and innocently thought Sarah Lee would be able to handle my win over her as graciously as I had accepted her ringlets as part of life with Sarah Lee.

A few days later, Sarah Lee's aunt was giving us a ride home from school. She was about to drop Sarah Lee off and asked me if I would like a ride home. At that point, Sarah Lee asked me to stay at her house and play. We got out of the car and walked toward her house, but as her aunt drove away Sarah Lee looked over her shoulder and said her mother had told her she couldn't play that day. I was struck dumb, in shock. Thoughts raced through my mind but nothing came out of my mouth. She didn't wait for me to recover as she turned and flounced into the house, chin turned up and those wretched curls bouncing down her back.

I walked my half-mile home, tears burning hot in my eyes, running down my cheeks. I felt hurt, embarrassed, angry, and, for some unknown reason, guilty about something. I plotted vengeance, felt betrayed, and vowed never to see her again. I walked home in a haze. When I arrived I didn't know what to say to my mother, so I mumbled something about there being a mixup and retreated to my room where I cried quietly and held my aching stomach. I had been taken advantage of and I felt violated and abused. My insides ached and I only wanted to curl up on my bed and cradle the soft and vulnerable feelings that had just been smashed.

This next experience reminds me of the story I so often hear when people explain why they don't sing—somewhere along the line some authority figure has told them they can't sing, or has suggested they be quiet because they aren't hitting the right note. My experience did not involve singing; it involved art. After this happened, I didn't paint or draw for twenty-three years.

In art class, I was given an assignment to copy a painting of a tree in watercolor. I was not able to conform to the picture that was presented to me, however. My tree's magnificent trunk grew out of wide-spread roots that joined with the earth in a partnership of security and appreciation. The branches reached into light and nourishment, radiating with brilliant colors. I was so pleased and proud. It was one of those moments of private pleasure that defies sharing. I couldn't wait for the teacher's confirmation of my suspicion that I had achieved a major breakthrough with my painting skills.

Instead, I received a distracted and annoyed look. My painting was brushed aside as not having fulfilled the assignment. My insides lurched and once again I withdrew, quietly and painfully, not knowing how to express what I felt. Something from deep within me was in that painting; for me it was not merely an exercise in artistic technique. I didn't know how to say this at the time, so I pulled back and didn't try to express myself through that avenue again. The pain of that incident was so deep that I could only lie on my bed at home and feel waves of hurt roll through my bowels and up and down my spine.

This went on for months and the pain was made worse by the fact that there was no one I could talk to about it. I tried to talk to my parents about it at first, but I only got a pat of sympathy on the head. When I tried again I got the supreme put-down and put-off: "You're being too sensitive, Carlin. Why do you always have to take things so personally? The teacher was just trying to help you. You have to be tougher." I wanted to scream at them but I lacked the words; only my rage was articulate. If I *had* had the words at the time they would have been something like, "Don't you know—I take criticism every day in all of my classes, from many friends, and from you and I handle it well, but this is different, this *feels* different, something in me has been violated, my insides have been abused, my sacred and vulnerable core has been threatened. That is important to me." Is this what you went through when someone told you you couldn't sing? Or did you quietly accept and forget the hurt, pushing it into a deep part of your less-conscious memory?

After such times of hurt I became quiet and withdrawn; I felt numb and removed. As I licked my wounds I would puzzle about why people would act as they did, or contemplate what I had done to provoke such an act, and ask God for guidance in protecting my sacred, vulnerable self from becoming scarred over or sealed up in armor for protection. I was told that I took things too hard and I suspect that was true. I also suspect it was true because I maintained my softness when others had already covered over theirs with so many layers of defense and emotional armor that they didn't remember any longer what their actions toward me might feel like. I didn't blame them; I simply believed they couldn't feel their own vulnerability anymore and presumed that I couldn't either.

Throughout this time, a part of me wanted to please the adults and conform as they wanted me to so I wouldn't be an embarrassment to them. One of the things that saved me from completely closing off my individuality and less conforming feelings was my habit of reading the biographies of important people. I was drawn to them and delighted in the interesting and often nonconforming lives they described. I noticed very quickly that people who were interesting enough to write about were rarely conforming children who did all of the "right" things. I concluded that I wasn't so "crazy" after all; perhaps only a little eccentric and stubborn. I now faced the dilemma of learning how to do what was right for me and not offend or frighten others.

The churches continued to draw me. (I didn't think this attraction was at all unusual at the time—it was only after I grew up and told people of my spiritual search that I thought it a bit unusual. At the time it seemed the most natural thing in the world to round out my education with more understanding and celebration of God in a church.) My only problem was in finding the "right" one. Because I had no family religious tradition to resort to, I took on the search myself. Somehow I felt that the answer to the pain I was experiencing in my life would be found in church.

My earliest memory of church was a visit to a "holy roller" service. The strongest image from this visit was of a large woman bowing and moaning something in front of a calendar with a picture of Jesus on it. I kept peeking around the lady beside me to see her giant polka dotted rear-end bobbing up and down as she wailed and sobbed inarticulate cries at the calendar. I asked what she was doing and was hushed with a quick, "She's praying." Oh, so that's what praying is, I thought. She sure didn't look too happy.

I also attended the Methodist, Baptist, Episcopalian, and Presbyterian churches. They were all within walking distance and not too alarming to my parents. My mother even went with me to the Presbyterian church a few times, but I went to the adult services at the Baptist church by myself. I would walk in briskly as if I was with someone who had just walked in so they wouldn't usher me to the Sunday School. I wore hat and gloves and just a touch of lipstick to make me look more mature. I wasn't about to go back to Sunday School, especially in the Baptist church, where I had heard they dunk kids all the way into a tank of water. I quit the Baptist church after listening to the minister spend the whole service talking love, love, love—I knew that he beat his kids, everyone at school knew, I think even the teachers knew. He only hit them under their clothing so it wouldn't show. Talk, talk, talk . . . words, words, words. Everyone was talking about love, but I didn't see much action. Where was the love really happening on this earth?

I spent a lot of time with adults at this time because I believed they had the answers I sought. I wanted them to be an example for me to follow. I would watch their actions and look for their happiness. Invariably, I only found a questioning look in their eyes. In fact, they seemed to be looking to me for something, too. What was it? I began to feel great intolerance for hypocritical grownups. I let go of feeling angry that they weren't setting a good example for me when I saw the humor in the idea that all of these adults were trying to fool God. Any God I could believe in would have to be able to see through adult games at least as well as I could. After all, an all-knowing God sees *all*. What a marvelous joke on everyone: there *is* no place to hide! I imagined God was chuckling away at all the games people were playing in an effort to keep Him happy. Or, perhaps they didn't even believe in God and were only pretending; in actuality, playing a great agreed-upon game where everyone is fooling everyone else. God must *really* be laughing at that one.

When I was thirteen I started taking catechism instruction at the local Catholic Church. It felt good. Finally, I was learning something. I had a private tutor, a nun, once a week for a whole year, free. They didn't know what else to do with a teenager who wanted to take eight years of catechism in one. I felt right at home. The nun was sweet and I didn't miss a single class. The lessons were easy, if a bit dull. I had nothing to prepare; I could simply go and spend time with this dear person each week for a whole hour, talking about God and love and peace of mind. The nun was so clean and starched and white, and I wondered if all nuns had flawless pink complexions like her. I loved her fresh look, her lack of jewelry or makeup, except the gold ring which meant she was a bride of Christ and therefore totally untouched. I felt I was in the presence of someone a bit otherworldly.

My family was sure I had gone a bit too far this time by joining the "idol worshippers." But I deeply enjoyed this being all mine—I didn't have to share it with anyone. No one understood anyway. I loved the sister and felt sadness when the year passed by so quickly. Although nothing really profound happened between us, the peace and gentleness communicated to me by another woman as a model for my blossoming femininity was priceless. I craved such a role model.and absorbed from her hungrily. At times I had words I wanted to share with her and questions left unasked, but I couldn't seem to express these feelings at the time. I was no longer so disturbed by the idea that no one could really understand my deep thoughts. In fact, I not only accepted this idea, I even came to believe I had nothing important to say anyway!

I joined the church and was baptized and confirmed. A magnificent bonus came with membership in this church: the priest was an exceptional musician and I was able to sing in the chorus. We sang all of the old Gregorian chants in Latin. The chants came so easily. The music flowed through me like a healing ray of light. I felt cleansed, even euphoric, while singing them. They seemed so familiar and comfortable. I broke through layers of shyness and self-consciousness in order to sing these chants. The priest appreciated my singing and seemed to approve of me also. I basked in being his "pet." I was the only young person in the choir.

The most wonderful thing about this church was that most of the Mass and all of the music and spoken responses were in Latin. I could drift off in bliss to a chorus of Latin mumble! The words, combined with the modal Gregorian chant wanderings, transported me to another state of consciousness. I would sometimes stop my participation to simply listen, feeling something stirring deep inside that pushed the tears up and out. No false, meaningless, manipulative words were spoken here; I was simply with people saying prayers, joined in a common purpose, feeling the oneness, letting go of our differences for that hour of celebrating the Mass. That's what we called it: a *celebration* of the Mass. We were joined together in the oneness of this celebration. No experts preached at us who thought they were intermediaries between God and me. (I'm sure that some of the priests had this illusion, but I didn't see it at the time.) I bathed in the single-mindedness of the Mass. The higher the Mass, the more music and ceremony it entailed, the more I loved it.

The ancient statues and paintings that adorned the

church spoke to me on other levels, different from words. The adoration of Mary spoke to my blooming womanhood with respect and honor, something I had begun to realize was sadly missing in my outside world as I felt men's eyes grabbing at my anatomy. "Blessed is the fruit of thy womb. . . ." That prayer gave my womb the right to holiness and dignity and balanced some of the confusion I felt in a world where the word for making love is also a curse and the words for sexual organs can also be used to condemn the whole person.

The church's artwork was well chosen and tasteful, and I got my first lessons in art appreciation from the same priest. I observed him carefully—his presence and actions had much to teach me. I thought of the artists who had created the exquisite pieces we had in that church and understood why I was so drawn to this art. There was more to those creations than beautifully designed ceramic molds and paint. The soul of the artist was speaking to me also. I looked deeply, and Mary's face changed and Jesus was so soft I wept, though I didn't know why.

The statues and paintings were draped and covered before Easter and I felt the loss sharply. My anticipation built through Holy Week and I delighted in the rush of feeling that ran from my toes to my overflowing tears on the Glorious White Light of Easter Morn as the veils came off and I saw these beloved statues once again with fresh eyes. They gleamed and sparkled and all seemed to be smiling. On this day, even Our Lady of Sorrows smiled. The pageantry of walking around the church with palm frond in hand, as others had done 2,000 years ago, as maybe I had done 2,000 years ago, touched me deeply. The tears welled up and I hid them because I still thought it was private business and no one would join me in these feelings.

At about this time my feelings reassured me that God does exist somewhere. These feelings helped me to remember what the pain so long ago had blocked. Through my tears, my perceptions opened once again, and my greatest fear emerged, the fear I had totally repressed from my conscious mind: maybe this is all a joke; there is no God. The adults know a secret and are keeping it from me, like Santa or the Tooth Fairy. But my feelings don't lie; they *know*. The "feeling" place in me talked without fear to the order of the universe. God and I took up a private, secret communion based on complete honesty and a great sense of humor. I finally felt a settling in and a contentment as the mother church nurtured me.

I went away to college and the church there was cold and hollow. It was time to let go of the church mother that had taught me so much and nurtured me so generously through my teens. The Catholic church slipped away quite easily. The gift of knowing that there was a connection to God remained deep in my heart as I peeled off layers of the business of religion and sorted out my thoughts about it.

I married with a baby in my womb and, at twenty-two, found myself repeating my own birth experience, now as the mother. After three days of labor my son Dane eased into life by way of a Caesarean section, unable to pass through a cervix frozen in fear and unconscious memory. With this soft bundle of freshness I felt something that I had never felt before. Each time I touched him the tears of joy overflowed. The exquisite feelings of joy and delight were so powerful that I almost moved away from them at times. I had never cared much for babysitting and didn't think that I had much in common with babies, but it felt so natural and easy with him. I was feeling love . . . love without anything else attached to it. There were no bargains, no plans, no contracts—only loving commitment, no matter what.

At this time a memory tried to penetrate my awareness: someplace else I had felt this love. It felt so clean, so clear, and so easy. I experienced a sinking feeling of guilt. I didn't feel this kind of love anyplace else—not with my family, friends, or husband. It was just there between Dane and me and I felt he knew it too. Who could I talk to about *this*? I felt so alone. I was in a cycle of rejecting the church, so I no longer had my nurturing church mother to go to. God was buried deep within me, awaiting rediscovery. Other mothers seemed so casual about their children. Were they feeling what I was feeling? I didn't think so. I couldn't even discuss this with my mother because we had not yet bridged the communication gap. I suspected that my mother knew about these tender, vulnerable feelings but somehow it wasn't something we could talk about. My heart ached with recognition whenever I saw her holding back her tears but the words weren't yet there to communicate with her about it. I also knew that my stepdad felt these feelings at times. I would catch a glimpse in his eyes but then he'd throw in some well-worn cliche, look away, and get busy not allowing any further entry into his soft, vulnerable place.

Thinking about that soft place of vulnerability triggers tears in my eyes even as I write this. What is this gentle and tender place within me? It seems to be located in the area of my stomach or solar plexus. It is the place feminist psychologists have dubbed the "hole," the empty place we try to fill with food and good deeds. Freud thought the empty place was our womb, empty of a penis or a child and aching for both to feel fulfilled. Why, then, does a married woman who has successfully borne children or a man who has no cavity in the first place also feel this empty space? Why do children feel this empty space long before they have ripened sexually? I feel that this empty space is the core of our innocence (not naivete—innocence). It is a sacred innocence, full of trust in the connection between us all.

We know somewhere in ourselves that we are all one and that what I do to you is also done to me. This is not the biblical eye for an eye, or the karma of doing a good act and getting one in return. It is simply the knowledge that as we give to one another we are at the same time giving to ourselves. The "soft place" is the place where we know all and are connected within infinite intelligence. This is the place where we know right from wrong for ourselves and for others as they relate to us. It is the psychic, intuitive center of our being that knows when someone is lying to us even though our mind provides no good reason for our suspicion. This is the place that won't let us lie to others or to ourselves for long. This is the place that is connected with all that has gone before and all that will come. This is the place that has compassion for the suffering of others, even though we can see how they bring it on themselves. This is the place of nonjudgment, a place of complete acceptance and trust. It is the place of faith in the order of the universe, the cycles of life and death, and the absence of duality.

We all have this soft, tender place; it responds to every event in our lives like a barometer does to weather changes. This place is wide open in some and quite closed in others, but it is in all of us and we choose how open or closed we want to be. When I am with people who are very open, I feel reverent, like I am in church and I want to be very quiet and gentle, speaking in whispers lest I disturb the sacred. When I am with people who have closed this place down, I feel a wall between us. I find myself saying too much in an effort to penetrate their barrier so we can communicate. But this is as effective as raising your voice to a foreigner in an attempt to improve communication.

This place in ourselves, where our sacred being resides, can become so blocked that only something grand or tragic can penetrate its sensibilities. One of the most common means for doing this is pain—physical, mental, emotional, spiritual, psychic, or whatever other form we choose. One of pain's effects is to stimulate us into action and it is very effective at this duty. Our entire culture only takes notice when pain appears, and then our only concern is to acquire a remedy to remove the pain.

It is important to realize that pain is a perfectly natural reaction which arises to help us deal more effectively with a problem. Our habitual response to pain can only serve us when we have learned to look for the lesson it offers. We can learn to recognize pain as an old friend who has returned to help us to know ourselves better, to help us go a little deeper into our awareness with its gift.

2 | Pain As Our Friend and Teacher

I would like to share some thoughts and insights I have gained from my experiences with pain. I will not solve the whole issue of pain, but will illustrate how we can take a belief such as "pain is bad" and turn it around to become "pain as a helpful tool" on our path of self-discovery.

I have lived with a lot of pain: mental, emotional, spiritual, and physical; thus, early in life I developed mechanisms to protect and guard myself against pain. I also hid the intensity of this pain from others out of a vague feeling of inexplicable guilt, a sense of it being "wrong" to be in so much pain. Unfortunately, this defense and resistance to pain created even more hurt in my life than the actual events themselves.

There came a time, however, when I began to view pain as a gift rather than an evil: pain eventually became my friend and teacher. I had been treating pain as an alarm to be shut off, though this was as unreasonable as thinking that a fire is extinguished by shutting off a fire alarm. Even though the alarm is silenced, the fire may still rage.

All pain, not just physical, became for me a warning system that alerted me to an imbalance somewhere in my being. Whereas before I would turn off the alarm with drugs or busy-ness, I began instead to let it ring, and listened more carefully to its message. Invariably, the pain led me to the specific area that wanted attention. I began to welcome the pain I had been avoiding. I also began to treat each painful event with respect instead of dismissing it as a mistake or an accident. Each time the pain occurred, I listened and tried to translate its messages. As I grew more skillful in understanding these messages, the pain alarm decreased in intensity. It seemed a tiny bell was enough; it no longer took a full, jarring alert to get my attention. I had moved gradually from a place where pain screamed within me to a place where pain was a gentle whisper in my ear. When I was not listening well, the whisper would increase in volume until I acknowledged the message and did something about it. At these times, there was no chance of missing the alarm message.

In the following sections, I will examine various common manifestations of pain so that you can learn to recognize your own pain alarms and how you presently turn these alarms off, as well as how you can open your reaction to pain so that you are able to learn what it has to teach you.

We will first look at physical pain, the most common and easy to identify. Next, we will address mental pain—difficulties that arise in our work, in our relationships, and in our very goals and ambitions. Anxiety is a primary expression of mental pain, and many emotional responses are triggered when our mind "runs away" with its fears.

Emotional pain, the third category, is often centered around loss—of a loved one, of security, or of self-esteem. Learning to allow ourselves the time to fully recover from an emotional trauma is a key ingredient in dealing effectively with this form of pain. The final category is spiritual pain—what I have come to call my "psychic ache." This is

most often encountered when we resist the call to grow spiritually and to respect the larger perspective of our life.

RECOGNIZING THE PAIN ALARM

For the fullest understanding, the pain to which I refer is not only physical, but also mental, emotional, and spiritual. Examples of each type follow:

Physical Alarms

Pain of the Body

Some of the most common symptoms include headache, diarrhea, constipation, allergy, indigestion, over- or underweight, and colds.

Alarm Shutoffs

Let your mind range for a moment over the amazing variety of over-the-counter-drugs available. All admit on the label that they relieve symptoms only, and warn us to see a doctor if symptoms persist. If these drugs fail and the condition worsens, we seek out a doctor who prescribes stronger remedies. Too often these are tranquilizers, pain pills, or amphetamines, frequently used in conjunction with our own prescriptions of street drugs and alcohol. These all treat symptoms. They do not cure anything. Consider, for example, our typical diet—high in fat and processed foods that have been robbed of their vital nutritive value. After eating a heavy meal, we often suffer stomach pain that we try to remedy with an antacid or some similar palliative. Eventually, after sustaining this eating pattern for years, we develop a more serious symptom such as gallstones, ulcers, or some other digestive-tract disturbance that requires surgery to remove the pain.

Had we known how to *listen* to the pain initially, and responded by changing to a healthier diet, we could have avoided this unfortunate turn of events. We also refuse to listen to our symptoms by keeping busy with our jobs, activities, and relationships so we can deny and suppress any messages physical pain may be trying to convey to us.

Getting the Message

A very generous man with a brain tumor told his story to thousands of people for years after his doctor told him that he had two weeks to live. He ended his story by saying, "I'm not going to have a doctor treating me who thinks I'm going to die in two weeks, so I fired him!" I heard the story many times and laughed along with the rest of the audience, but each time I was struck by the hushed quality of the laughter. It was as if we should not be laughing at the doctor. Our storyteller was admired as a hero for his bravery. And what was his heroic deed? It was simply standing up to his doctor and not accepting the prognosis of "two weeks to live" as the last word on his condition. This seems to me a graphic example of how we usually look up to experts and overlook their frailties.

This story is not a new one, however. Examples abound of people who recovered from serious illness in spite of dire predictions, and of people who died for no known medical reason. The point is, we need to accept that our health is primarily our individual responsibility. Part of this responsibility entails demanding appropriate care from our chosen health-care professional. We can insist that our healing specialist provides more than symptomatic relief. If we aren't satisfied with one, we can seek another. We have a right to physical health and can certainly shop around if we feel we are not getting the treatment that will help balance our system. We do not have to accept a diagnosis that is merely a label for the ailment, or treatment of the symptoms alone, or a lifetime of increasingly severe relapses and decreasing hope.

Appropriate counsel from healing specialists is available and we can use these caring and specialized people (who have studied long and hard to help us) as we would a reference book in the library. We can shop around, ask for options, go elsewhere when our feelings tell us we're in the wrong place. After all, how ironic it is that the same person will on one day shop at six stores and give sales-clerks fits until just the right TV or pair of shoes is selected, and yet, on the next day, accept without question one specialist's opinion that a piece of their anatomy should be removed!

When I shop for my healing helper, I want someone who sees me as more than a malfunctioning body. I want someone who treats my ulcer symptoms and goes on to ask me about my relationships, recent life changes, children, work—perhaps even my spiritual philosophy. This isn't idle chit-chat; after all, it is my entire lifestyle that is contributing to the message my stomach is attempting to communicate by its malfunction.

This may sound a bit ideal, but don't give up. Wonderful healing helpers are out there, waiting to be appreciated and encouraged. I don't require this kind of wholeness in everyone who helps me. If I want a wart removed I don't insist that the doctor be a spiritual analyst as well, but if I want to learn more about my being, I will not stop with a simple wart removal procedure, either. I will go on to learn more about what my body is trying to teach me by growing warts.

The prospect of being our own healer sounds much more frightening than it really is. In fact, we are already doing it, even though we may be involved with (and surrendering to) many specialists. We are participating in our healing process even by selecting the specialist. We do have a choice and this is no accident. In my opinion, this is one of the reasons for so many suits against medical practitioners. We feel guilty about putting so much trust for our own well-being in another; then, when they don't perform like gods we lash out at them in anger and *get* them! I have tremendous respect for skilled people. I seek them out. And I remember that no matter how skilled,

they are people just like me who have their own life traumas which may influence their judgments involving the
problems I take to them.

I feel it is my responsibility to continually monitor what
is right for me.

Mental Alarms

Pain of the Mind

We often get caught up in our duty to our work and our
mental logic prevents us from hearing the messages about
this problem, though it may be obvious to observers.
Some of the most common symptoms include: not wanting to get up and go to work, frequent accidents on the job
that lead to a loss of work time, fear of job loss, feelings of
stress with boss or co-workers, dread of certain tasks at
work, worrying about work at home, taking out work
stress on family members, using work as the excuse for
behavior away from work, spending many extra hours at
work trying to do it right, feeling singled out at work for
extra duty, and using work as an excuse to neglect other
areas of your life.

Alarm Shutoffs

We respond to most of our mental alarms with intellec-
tualization and rationalization, telling ourselves, for example, that it is "natural" to dislike work; everyone has at
some time. Some of these rationalizations are: work is a
duty, my job pays well and I shouldn't complain, I need the
money, and I am already trained for this job so a change
would waste this training.

Getting the Message

One-third of your life will be spent at work; thus, it is important to protect this investment. You do not have to accept working conditions that are not suitable to your

individual mental needs. Your mental needs are uniquely yours. One person's personality and temperament may be able to handle stress that would be impossible for another. There are many ways to shift mental stress without changing jobs. If the job seems worth keeping, you can work less days, change hours, departments, desks, stores, or do some of the work in another location.

Make a list of the working conditions that would suit you mentally and match them with your present job and a possible future one. Get unstuck. Talk to friends who seem happy in their work. Is it their job, or their attitude? Don't resign yourself to an uncomfortable situation. There is always another way. Don't give up.

Get a boost from someone who likes and believes in you. Let them help you to recover your self-respect and find a job worthy of your skills. Ask a professional helper. Perhaps you are really suited by temperament for another profession. Staying in a job because you have the training is *not* a good enough reason.

I have met many people who, like myself, have quit active and productive professions in order to enjoy life more. Though I had been effective and successful in others' eyes, I felt I was straining beyond comfort levels. I am now using my skills in ways which suit my mental makeup perfectly for this time in my life. To another, however, the "stress" from my present work might prove unbearable.

Emotional Alarms

Pain of the Heart

One of the most common causes of emotional pain is the loss of a lover or mate. When this happens we may feel rejected, lonely, anxious, depressed, unable to sleep, lethargic, and bored. We often fantasize about our mate being sexual with another, feel hostile and even violent toward the person who ended the relationship, experience uncomfortable anger or even feel suicidal or murderous. We may experience a loss of appetite, a mental restlessness, or inability to concentrate. We cry easily and are unable to stop thinking about the situation. Our attempts to feel loving toward the person who left fail. This pain can be equally acute for the one who has left, especially if they are feeling guilty about this decision.

Alarm Shutoffs

Often we get really busy, or we may sleep with others for acceptance or approval. We might gravitate rapidly to another partner/mate and live together or marry as soon as possible. We may try to arrange for our former lover to see us having a good time with someone else, or at least make sure the story gets back to the "ex." We may take alcohol and drugs, use perfume and makeup, lose weight, wear sexier clothing, and/or move to a new place.

Getting the Message

The vital role of patience in healing is, perhaps, most needed, yet most ignored, in the case of emotional problems. We need time to regain our perspective. We also need to recognize that we are emotionally wounded so we can treat our wound with the same care and respect we would give to treating a physical condition such as a broken bone or pneumonia.

Seek objective counsel from friends or a healing specialist. Insist that those who would support you cultivate a positive attitude toward your cycle of anger, mourning, and recovery. After all, you have a right to emotional health, to get help to create a program that will maintain this health, and a plan for handling relapses. If you don't feel movement toward emotional peace within a reasonable length of time, find another helper. Trust your intuition to guide you to a helper who will value your emotional health as you do, and who will rejoice with you when you achieve and maintain emotional balance.

The end of a relationship can be a wonderful opportunity to learn more about yourself. Stay alone for awhile, gathering the strength you need to achieve wholeness. Spend more time with friends who are not potential sexual partners. Be honest with new acquaintances—tell them that you are healing emotionally, as you would if you were healing physically. It takes awhile to rebalance and remember that all decisions are mutual. And don't worry about sexual relations—this will come naturally and easily when you are fully recovered.

At one time I felt so raw and jangled emotionally that when I wrote down the goals I had for my emotional health, all I could think of was the word "calm." "Please, dear universe," I implored, "grant me a moment of emotional calm."

Spiritual Alarms

Pain of the Soul

Some of the most common symptoms of spiritual problems include: having no trust in the worth of life, feeling dull, languid, depressed, or often quite the opposite— feeling absolutely euphoric and wonderful when there is no good reason to feel this way. Life can be chaotic or the physical world may appear to be in disarray. We may have visions, hear voices, see colors around people and objects, dream someone has died at the actual moment of their death. We may feel drawn to express ourselves spiritually, even though we want nothing to do with organized religions. I have experienced a deep pain that I call my "psychic ache." I know it is not of physical, mental, or emotional origin. It is an undeniable ache that tells me I am veering off my spiritual path and it does not disappear until I right the imbalance in my life.

Alarm Shutoffs

Often our reaction to these alarms is to try and hide them through denial, suppression, or projection, because we fear being labeled "crazy." Or we may go from specialist to

specialist in the areas of mental and physical health trying to find cures. The specialists may do their best, yet the
pain continues.

Getting the Message

Accept unexplainable phenomena as gifts from other levels of awareness that can help with your perspective on
life. A simple, delightful opening takes place when we acknowledge that more than five senses may be working for
us. Share with others who have had similar happenings.
Seek out a spiritual group. If their style doesn't suit you,
shop around. I have known many religious leaders who
have had experiences they don't always share with their
congregations yet are happy to discuss such experiences
with a kindred soul.

If you fear the opinion of others, remember that those
who think you are crazy may be afraid to open to their
own awareness and feel threatened when you do. Perhaps
they are simply afraid rather than being against you. The
attitude of acceptance you cultivate will flow out to others
and help them to feel comfort also. And even if you and I
were crazy . . . what is crazy? Are you harming anyone or
threatening society? I know a person in his late seventies
who was institutionalized years ago. He escaped and has
been a street puppeteer ever since under an assumed
name. He has charmed and delighted multitudes, received acclaim from citizens' groups, supported himself,
and is still going strong. What a waste to have him locked
away and drugged by his caretakers. And yes, he is a bit
crazy, by any standards, but delightfully so.

I have a clear memory of an experience I had when I was
five that I have come to think of as my first spiritual revelation. I was watching ants in a large ant hill with complete absorption and fascination, fantasizing about what
it must be like inside . . . when it occurred to me that we
are like the ants. We dash around in cars, going to work
and coming home, or at play, but always busy, on the
move, like the ants, and someone big could be looking at
us, like I watched the ants, and we might never even know

it! I thought, maybe there *is* a god, and I looked to the sky and knew there was no end and wondered where the big giant would stand to watch us. I stepped carefully after this. . . .

Years later, sitting at my high school biology microscope, I recalled the ant hill as I looked at cells dashing about and my thoughts jumped out to deep space to watch planets and stars executing their own dance. And my awe at the magnificent order of the universe was rekindled once more.

Body, mind, emotions, and spirit are not really separated, so imbalances that occur within our system often overlap one another. For example, have you noticed that when your body is injured or ill, your mind doesn't function very well either? When you are under an emotional strain, is it difficult to concentrate on your work?

Although we have done our best to isolate functions in order for experts to specialize, this separation is only illusion. You are the finest expert and authority on what is best for your entire being and nothing can surpass your own knowledge, intuition, and sense of timing about what is best for you. You know what is best for your being's full health; thus, you are the ultimate healer.

A SUGGESTED PROGRAM FOR HEALTH MAINTENANCE

The following are some guides to easing our symptoms and maintaining our equilibrium. These suggestions take us beyond the simple act of shutting off alarms and help us to treat the whole being. These preventative measures cross over any imaginary boundaries between body, mind, emotions, and spirit. This is the advice I'd like to get from a doctor:

WALK. Walking is the most underrated form of therapy, probably because there is no money in teaching it and no special clothes are needed to do it. Nonetheless, I did recently see a walking group advertised at a pretty hefty fee.

Aren't we wonderfully silly at times? We pay someone to wash our car and mow our lawn, then pay someone else to make us stretch and bend. This is not entirely bad; if we pay someone a fee we are more likely to make a commitment, and group energy *is* stimulating.

Walk empty-handed; wear comfortable clothing and shoes. Walk through neighborhood streets, by the water, up and down hills. Wherever it pleases you to walk will be just fine. Let your walking be easy—no striving. Walk thirty to sixty minutes daily, alone or with a comfortable companion with whom you won't talk too much. Enjoy the silence and the feel of your body in rhythm. Breathe, chest up, shoulders down and relaxed, put a spring in your step.

AFFIRMATIONS.   Affirmations are simply statements about our condition that are stated in the *present* and stated positively. Examples: I am healthy, I am overflowing with vigor and life, my blood pressure is exactly right for me (or in the "normal" range), my relationships are full of unconditional love and comfort, my sexuality is rich and full and my sexual sharing is easy and delightful, I eat only what is healthy for my body/mind, I run two miles a day, I love and respect myself.

Sometimes it is hard to state our present condition in such positive terms, particularly if we are not feeling good about how we are conducting our lives. We continually program ourselves, often with negative input: "I'm lazy and never finish anything on time," "I'm too fat," "I'll never be able to quit smoking," and so on.

Affirmations reverse this negative process. When making an affirmation, we state it in positive terms, as if it is already happening: "I am slender and full of energy," "I finish my projects on time or even ahead of schedule," or "My lungs are pink and clean and only take in health and nourishment from my world."

LET GO.   Use the "Bridge of Release" or the "Leaf in the Water" daily, or even hourly if you feel you are carrying an excessively heavy load. (Both are described in Chapter Six of this book, page 103.

MEDITATE. This is not a mysterious occult process; basically, it is a way of connecting with something larger than us. How you do it is not as important as making the connection. Chapter Six, which is on meditation, will help you get a start.

RELAX. Deep relaxation can be very simple, if practiced faithfully. I learned this from my Auntie Jo when I was a child. Later it was taught to me as an esoteric ritual leading to self-hypnosis. The combination of modern technique and Auntie Jo's sleep suggestions goes like this:

> As you lie down, talk to your feet, tell them to relax . . . see them as wanting to obey your wishes and feel them absorbing the power of relaxation into every fiber of their being. Continue up your body in as much detail as your knowledge of anatomy allows. Also ask the mind, emotions, spirit to surrender to this moment of letting go.

This is done very nicely in conjunction with the "Bridge of Release" image.

VISUALIZE. Set the stage with great care for this exercise. See yourself in a place of great comfort. It can be a place of great beauty and peace, someplace you remember or something you make up right now. Bring into your scene another being, someone familiar, someone famous from history, or from the future or outer space, or not a person at all. This being will be your Inner Healer, available to you at all times as your healing helper. Tell that person/being about the help you need. Listen for the answer (there is more on listening in Chapter Six).

We respond holistically to an image, whether we consciously decide to respond or not. When I tell students in my yoga class to move into a certain position, they are actually able to attain this position more easily if I also tell them to relax and move gracefully. When I tell them to imagine they are a grand old tree swaying gently in the wind, however, they become grace itself. An image speaks equally to our body, mind, and spirit, and we respond fully.

INTEND.   When we clarify our intentions, our body, mind, and spirit all work together, in harmony. When we fail to be clear about our intentions, we may find ourselves spending all our energy trying to achieve what we *think* we want. For example, if our mind has decided that we will lose weight, but our body craves calories in spite of this intention, we need to look to our whole selves for the appropriate answer.

A good way to clarify your intentions is to write your goals down, decide on a deadline for accomplishing these goals, and, at the end of the time period, review the goals and evaluate what you have achieved in this time. Those goals you have accomplished will reveal the times you have been clear in your intention, and those you have failed to achieve will point out the areas where you need to be clearer with yourself about your goals.

To clarify my intentions, I make five columns, headed: Physical, Mental, Emotional, Spiritual, and Other (the Other category captures goals that may not fit into any of the other four categories). Then, starting with the Physical category, I think about what my ideal physical state of being would be, and note whatever this would involve in the Physical column. I do the same for the other categories as well.

Once, when I was doing this process, I noted under Physical that my teeth were white, shining, and healthy (for twenty-five years one of my front teeth had been badly discolored from a root canal). I forgot the list in the coming months, until, one day, during a routine dental visit, the dentist replaced the tooth with a cap because he felt it was "too fragile." My medical insurance even covered the cost!

Thus, I had achieved my goal of white, shining, healthy teeth without even consciously working toward it. By stating my desire, I had created a focus that my whole being could align itself with.

WRITE. Use a diary or journal in which to record thoughts, feelings, things you may not want to share with others. If you are worried that it will be read by others, lock it away—this way you will feel secure enough to express your deepest feelings without inhibition. I have learned to appreciate so many more dimensions of my being by writing in this way.

APPRECIATE. In our society, we are taught to think we are vain if we love ourselves. I had spent time talking about "loving myself" and had even shared the importance of this concept with students for many years, but there never seemed to be any real "zing" in the idea. The "zing" always seemed to be reserved for that someone special, not for myself.

One night as I was driving home from a yoga class, listening to the radio, feeling good, a rush of love swept through me. I had no special lover at the time and was not thinking of anyone else. Then it suddenly dawned on me what I was feeling. It was a rush of love for myself. I pulled over to the side of the road and wept at the beauty of asking for what I wanted and receiving it with my whole heart.

Take stock of all of your blessings. *No one can truly appreciate you like you can.* See yourself as lovable and valuable. Gen, a dear friend and teacher for my youngest son, had her children walk through doorways saying, "I am lovable and valuable," and look into mirrors saying, "I love myself unconditionally." What do you say when you look at yourself in a mirror? Allow yourself to feel the fullness of your gratitude. I suspect that a person who doesn't experience gratitude won't experience love either.

ACCEPT. We are such an "aspirin" society, taught to dodge pain since we were born, and wanting instant relief from any discomfort. The fastest route is not always the best. There is time to shop . . . don't panic. Look to your discomfort as a sign to get off the self-destructive track and onto a more healthful way of being in the world.

SMILE.   Keep your sense of humor or develop one. When I can't laugh at myself I know I am off center.

TRUST.   Our body/mind cycles in and out of life/death every second of our lives. Don't give in to the belief that you have irreparably set in motion something you can't change. You are not stuck. You can choose again, and start off in a new direction.

PRACTICE.   Rather than trying to change old patterns that don't work, create new ones and practice them. Some of our less-conscious belief systems are acquired even before our memory recalls, and can be running our lives and motivating our behavior whether we acknowledge them or not. I think it is nearly impossible to go back and attempt to dislodge all of our old habit patterns. But I do feel it is possible to start a new habit. Practice it as many times as needed to override the old. Practice the new habits with the discipline and devotion of a fine musician. Diligent practice will override the old conditioning.

TOUCH.   We tend to use words in an attempt to intellectually join. Touching can be an even more effective way to connect. Imagine how much more comfortable a visit to a sick person would be if we talked less and touched more. Most people, whether confined or not, are delighted with a shoulder rub or hand massage. It is such a simple gift of pleasure and connection that we always carry with us.

OTHERS.   The above suggestions are some basic methods I've discovered to nurture my wholeness. Many other means exist as well; some are already popular in our culture, including diet, environment, exploring our creativity, and music. Take a moment to notice the times when you have felt deep peace of mind and harmony with the whole world. Note these times and the circumstances and appreciate yourself for providing these moments of connection in your life. In my work, I enjoy the privilege of showing people their beautiful facets which they have previously ignored.

GETTING ACQUAINTED WITH PAIN AS A FRIEND

The following exercise has helped me to understand my feeling-level response to pain or problems, whether physical, mental, emotional, or spiritual. I have demonstrated this exercise to thousands of people over the years in classes and workshops, and it is always a delight to witness so much self-discovery in action. I thank my friends in Aikido for the gift of this process. The procedure may sound familiar to natural birth participants who have practiced relaxing with pain.

DIRECTIONS: This exercise requires two people. Aaron lies on his back, one forearm raised, elbows on the floor. Josh holds Aaron's wrist, and bends his hand forward until Aaron feels pain. (No heroics here—this is not a test to see how brave you are—just allow yourself enough pain to test out the idea.) Aaron will nod when he is ready to start and will tap on the floor with his free hand as a sign for Josh to stop. Three separate responses can be made to the pain and they should follow the order given below:

1. Resisting/Avoiding. First, Aaron resists Josh's pressure on the hand both physically and mentally by tensing up. Josh stops when Aaron taps.
2. Distracting/Ignoring. Next, Aaron does not resist either mentally or physically, but simply thinks of something else, such as counting the dots or cracks

in the ceiling. Josh starts to increase the pressure and stops when Aaron taps.

3. Blending/Joining. Josh guides Aaron into a relaxed state by encouraging him to breathe deeply and visualize something relaxing. (Suggestions: breathing a favorite color throughout the body, feeling peace of mind, feeling a blending and joining with Josh, asserting that Josh is offering a *gift* of pain to Aaron and this pain will spread throughout Aaron's body/ mind.)

Aaron nods when ready, Josh starts pressure, releasing when Aaron taps or when Josh feels like stopping, whichever comes first. Aaron and Josh talk about the different sensations experienced during the three stages of the exercise. Both will probably have much to share from their differing points of view. Aaron and Josh then change roles and repeat the exercise.

The following statements include both my own experiences and those shared by others after doing the exercise:

1. Resistance: "My whole body was involved in the response."

"I felt afraid and angry."

"Ann's tap on the floor was a slap and she made a sound this time."

"The anticipation was as bad as the pain."

"I felt competition with my partner, didn't want her to cause me pain . . . I realized how this fits in my life . . . I protect myself from others hurting me all the time."

2. Distraction: "My hand went down farther."

"It still hurt but not as sharply."

"I could count the ceiling tiles only so long until the pain overwhelmed me."

"Reminds me of a trip to the dentist and my mother telling me to think of something else as the shot went in."

"Is this like hypnosis?"

"I can do this forever and not feel pain until the last moment."

"This is how I always deal with a problem—I ignore it."

"This reminds me of noticing a bruise and not knowing what I was doing when I got it . . . my mind must have been absorbed elsewhere."

3. Blending:

"I had a lot of time with this one . . . I could decide when to tap, there seemed to be no urgency."

"I didn't feel the pain as much."

"I didn't want to press any harder on my partner's hand, he seemed to not feel it at all . . . I finally just stopped."

"My hand went down much farther this time before I tapped."

"I followed the pain, like a little guide through a tunnel."

"I could feel the joining with my partner, as if she was taking some of my pain."

"I just got in touch with my lower back pain. I have been letting my lower back do all of the work that my legs should be doing."

"I have never allowed myself to go with pain . . . this is amazing. I really am in charge."

Classifying different types of pain and the contrasting responses to it is a revelation to most of us. We usually

limit ourselves to one category for pain: "bad." My usual
first response to pain and problems is resistance, as in
the first part of the pain exercise. I take up a defensive
stance and ready myself to "reject it," lock the door, stop
it, do something to halt its progress *now!* And it has occurred to me that I create (or at least intensify) most of my
pain with this resistance and anticipation alone. Learning this has enabled me to make some dramatic shifts in
the way I allow pain (emotional, mental, spiritual, and
physical) into my life.

When I run from a possibly painful encounter, I alter
my whole life to avoid it. My resistance requires planning;
if I choose to ignore a problem by ducking out of the door,
not answering the phone, not returning a call, or drug-
ging myself, some degree of premeditation is certainly
called for. Both resisting and ignoring, as in the first and
second ways of addressing pain, require a great deal of
defensive maneuvering *before* the pain/problem can get
anywhere near me. Moreover, my efforts to resist this situation actually magnify the intensity of pain in the situation. Whenever the situation recurs, I am forced to act
immediately to avoid the pain.

This is the chief cause of my stress and it is very tiring.
It is a controller's game of getting all of the dominoes lined
up just right; it guarantees tension in the process and
anger when a domino falls the wrong way. When those
lined-up dominoes are people in our lives whom we are
attempting to control, we are setting ourselves up for
much pain and confusion.

However, when I can accept the pain in a situation,
when I am able to open to it and blend with it, I have
ample time to center myself so that I can better deal with
the problem. When I can view a problem from this perspective, and believe that I have the strength to weather
the difficulties, then each successive wave of trouble that
knocks me over in actuality makes me stronger and more
capable.

Let's further clarify how pain and separation are partners. We know a lot about how pain causes discomfort, and we understand a little about how separation can cause pain. We are less aware of how this separation occurs in the first place and how some subtler forms of separation that we accept and even encourage may be causing us tremendous confusion and pain. Some of these forms are *labeling, comparing, ranking,* and *categorizing.* Think for a moment about how we use each of these in our lives:

- What do we promote when we *label* a person, place or thing? Does it bring the results we really desire? For example, when I label my boss as "impossible," I will reinforce that label at every opportunity. This will only cause a gap to widen between us. Although I may have originally created the label out of frustration, I now find that the label itself has only served to increase that frustration, and to decrease the hope of ever establishing good communication with my boss.

- What do we help bring about emotionally in our mates when we *compare* them to others? Will I really improve my relationship with my husband by comparing him to someone "better"? Or will I only reinforce his feelings of inadequacy and thus undermine our relationship even further?

- What do we set in motion when we *rank* and file a child? When I, as an adult, talk down to a child—berating, criticizing, and communicating to that child that he or she is not worthwhile—what is the message I am really conveying to the child? Am I communicating love and acceptance that will foster that child's security and ability to love, or am I setting in motion a lifetime pattern for the child of insecurity, an inability to love, and continual low self-esteem?

- What do we cultivate in ourselves when we *judge* others? When I judge others and find them wanting, what does this say about my self-image? Do I really

believe that I am perfect? Do I even want to be perfect? Do I want to create a world where everyone will
be measured against my standards and will always be
found lacking?

- How do we serve our world when we *categorize* a
  whole race or ethnic group? If we lump an entire
  group of people into a category, it is far easier to dis-
  pense with them, to consider them less important
  than we are ourselves. This thinking paves the way
  for national and racial tensions which will ultimately
  lead to war. Is this the best way to serve the world?

Any of these traits may prevent us from knowing another's full potential. We also severely limit the way we can
relate to someone. And certainly in all the above cases we
guarantee *separation* from others.

When a word like "prejudice" goes out of style, we assume the practice has passed on also, but biases are still
alive and flourishing, though perhaps in less obvious (or
at least less well-recognized) forms. And these biases are
still doing the same damage, not so much to the party
being judged as to the judgment-makers themselves.

In the pain exercise given above we can experience an
erasing of our pain in the third way of addressing pain,
when we *join* with our partner. Separation is a defensive,
reactive measure designed to protect us from presumed
hurts by exposure to negativity. Joining is an assertive
and welcoming gesture designed to open us to presumed
good will.

When I open myself to joining with the problem/pain
from the start, as in the third stage of the pain exercise,
I have an entirely different perspective. For one thing, I
gain a most important element: *time.* During the time
that lapses between the presentation of a problem and my
reaction, I can now relax, breathe, and prepare myself to
receive the lesson. When I was resisting or ignoring pain
or problems, I had to spend that same amount of time in
panic, setting up barricades to protect myself. Now, when
I hear my mind racing with plans to control my problem, I

stop and remember that I can choose how I want to re-spond: my problem may be dealt with as an obstacle or a delightful lesson. I have a choice. My old habitual patterns still come up *and* I have a new way which is becoming my *new* habitual response, even in emergency situations. The calm exterior is now matched with an equally calm interior, and I am not experiencing an emergency alert with every little happening in my life.

3 Belief Systems

People often ask me how I have gotten my life into such a peaceful place, particularly in light of the pain I lived with for so many years. The first step was to examine my belief systems and decide whether they served me or enslaved me and the second was to realize that I had a choice. Belief systems can be very helpful, too. We can learn to use them as guides, much as a captain would use a lighthouse to guide his ship to safety in the fog.

As long as I use these tools while they serve me and let them go when they are no longer useful, I am fine. Problems arise, however, when I rely on my belief systems to provide the ultimate answer. These problems increase when I decide my belief systems are appropriate for all future decisions. And when I think my belief systems are right for everyone else, I have become their servant.

Let our belief systems be vehicles to set us in motion . . . not our destination.

Any pain I presently experience is directly related to the strength of my expectations. When they are too rigidly defined, I have to remind myself constantly that there are unlimited ways to approach any problem and limitless resources to deal with it. When I forget and find myself stuck in a corner, I have to reach out and say, "Help! Is there anyone out there who is able to see another way to do this?"

One way of working with belief systems is to view them as temporary, like a pair of shoes that will wear out. Don't be afraid to try on new ones. A belief system can help organize your thoughts and feelings for a time. Ask of your belief system that it contain some basic universal truth, no exclusivity and no separation. For the most part, it is not our conscious belief systems that cause us the most pain and confusion, but our subtler, less-conscious belief systems. These are the belief systems we are seldom aware of, though they influence most of our everyday attitudes toward life. They are beliefs we grew up with, and we assume everyone else shares them. Less-conscious belief systems form the underpinnings of reality as we define it in our present culture. At one point in history, less-conscious belief systems perpetuated the idea that the world was flat. Such beliefs are usually operating behind the scenes when we make remarks like: "I really don't see how he could do a thing like that," or "I could never do such a thing."

The following scenario for a play is the heart of this book. I wrote it a few years ago to share a good laugh at myself with friends. It is about how I have been caught in so much confusion and pain in my life. Now I share it with you also, in good humor, and hope you will join me in a good laugh at ourselves and our belief systems. The intent of the play is not to make fun of others, but to delight in the more comic side of those human failings so common to us all.

PROGRAM

The Label Game

or

A Pain For All Reasons

by

C. MOST HUMANKIND

a play in
3 Acts

ACT I

Scene 1   The Set-up
Scene 2   The Reinforcer

ACT II

Scene 1   Allies, White Hats, and Us
Scene 2   Teaching the Ignorant, Saving Souls
Scene 3   Devaluation of the Others

INTERMISSION

ACT III

Scene 1   Treading on the No-nos
Scene 2   Reservations for Reverence
Scene 3   Venerable Veneration

THE END

EXIT

or

INTERMISSION

BRIDGE TO A NEW BEGINNING

Scene 1   Reversing the Pedestals
Scene 2   Befriending the Sacred Cows

EPILOGUE

Peace of Mind Goes With Me

STAGING OUR OWN
MELLOW-DRAMA:

The margin comments
are 'asides,' an old
theatre tradition to
clarify underlying
motives

A PAIN FOR ALL REASONS

in Three Acts

with

Optional Bridge and Epilogue

To

Examine the Effects of Separation

ACT I

Scene 1: The Set-up

DIRECTIONS: *Carefully build, or become aware of, a belief system,* hereafter referred to as B.S.
A B.S. must have:
—Logic
—Investment

fear is the
incentive here

—Assumption
—Expectation
—Self-fulfilling prophecy

EXAMPLES:
"My children will make me proud."
"This is my mate for life."
"I'm too old for that."
"I'm not smart enough."

very subtle
separation begins
to creep in

"If I get my feet wet, my resistance will go down, germs will attack me, and I'll get sick."
(blank spaces below to fill in your own)

_____

_____

Scene 2: The Reinforcer

DIRECTIONS: Add *past experience* and *cause and effect* for support so you won't waver.

EXAMPLES: (you fill in the blanks):
   "My mother/father always said,

_____

_____ "

   "In my family we did _____ "

   "I always _____ "

   "I never _____ "

   (room to add more)

   "_____ "

   "_____ "

ACT II

Scene 1: Allies, the White Hats, and Us

DIRECTIONS: Gather people around us to support our B.S. We call them:
   "Friends"
   "Intelligent"
selective joining   "Sensitive"
   "Spiritually superior"
   "Comfortable to be with"
   (your turn to add a few)

_____

_____

Scene 2: Teaching the Ignorant, Saving Souls

DIRECTIONS: Teach *them* our B.S. We call *them*:

separation

"Students"
"Clients"
"Patients"
"Children"
(keep smiling and add several, if you want)

_____

_____

Scene 3: Devaluation of the Others

DIRECTIONS: *Devalue* those who persist with their own B.S. We call *these*:

now we are into *more
obvious separation
(Notice the little star.
We may visit this
section once again.)

"Dumb"
"Unevolved"
"Impossible to reason with"
"Delinquent"
"Retarded"
"Incomprehensible"
"Parents"
"Bums"
"He was an accident"
"Following some jerk"
(want to add a few? . . . there are plenty more)

_____

_____

INTERMISSION

Give yourself 10 minutes to absorb the above and prepare for a delightful third act.

ACT III

Scene 1: Treading on the No-nos

DIRECTIONS: Look for the *experts* we listen to, respect, value, esteem, and appreciate. We call *them*:
"Professional"
"Teacher"
"Licensed"
"Minister"
"Psychic"
"Master"
"Ph.D."
"Guru"
"Therapist"
(you may need an extra page to add on here)

more separation plus fear in the well-disguised form of admiration

_____

_____

Scene 2: Reservations for Reverence

only Gibran could say this in palatable form: "What shall I say of a man who slaps me when I kiss him on the face and who kisses my foot when I slap him?"

DIRECTIONS: Look for the *martyrs* we worship, extol, laud, and exalt. We call *them*:
"Saint"
"Such a hard worker"
"Angel"
"Unselfish"
"Blessed"
(only a few more to go)

_____

_____

Scene 3: Venerable Veneration

DIRECTIONS: Look for the *miracles and miracle-workers* we glorify, hail,

venerate, honor, and acclaim. We call
them:

we start with awe and
cover fast with our
censor and critic . . .
either way setting
them apart with
thoughts that we can't
do what they can

"Act of God"
"Child prodigy"
"82-year-old jogger"
"Self-made millionaire"
"Highly evolved"
"Bank robber"
"Healer"
"Amazing"
(do you dare to add on here?)

FURTHER DIRECTIONS: Our play can end
here with a conscious, or, more often,
less-conscious choice.

THE END

Stop here, content with a "system of
organizing our world and finding
comfortable labels for ourselves." We
jump onto the game board, assuming
our "role" in life. We continue with
logical reasons for our labels and
much justification, easily documented
with a little help from our Act II
"Allies," for staying where we are at
least for the time being.

INTERMISSION

EXIT or Reflection time before going on the BRIDGE

BRIDGE: A NEW BEGINNING

Scene 1: Reversing the Pedestals

breaking into our
own B.S.

DIRECTIONS: Return to ACT II immediately! Go to "Those we have *devalued* or who persist with another B.S." and pick one that stands out especially strongly. Take your selection through the *phase-one experience*:

1. Experience them anew . . . see them with new eyes . . . accept their credibility for just one instant.

reluctant joining

2. See them as teachers . . . as perfect . . . listen to them with the same awe usually reserved for ACT III performers (Experts, Martyrs, and Miracle Workers).

3. Look into their mirror for a reflection of the facets of our being that are asking for recognition.

FURTHER DIRECTION: Take plenty of time here . . . many old habits will attempt blockage . . . wait them out. If you feel confused, take a break, and perhaps repeat Phase One at a later date. If you feel stimulated and still have your sense of humor intact, please continue.

Scene 2: Befriending the Sacred Cows

DIRECTIONS: Return to ACT III

CHARACTERS: the *Experts, Martyrs, and Miracle Workers*. Pick one from each Scene that is especially

treasured. Take your selection
through the *phase-two experience.*

1. See the *Expert* defined as
   someone who:
   - Tells us to trust them with what
     we don't trust in ourselves.
   - Will confirm our ideas and give
     us acceptance.
   - Has been deemed an *Expert* by
     other *Experts.*

2. See the *Martyr* defined as
   someone who:
   - Does something we don't want
     to do.

3. See the *Miracle-worker* as
   someone or something that:
   - Breaks through our B.S.

4. Experience each one anew . . .
   from a different viewpoint . . .
   reverse some of the adoration.

5. Become aware of the share of the
   partnership they are fulfilling by
   their role. What strengths or
   weaknesses are their roles
   encouraging in us?

6. Look into their mirror reflection
   for the facets of our being that
   are asking for recognition.

more reluctant joining

EPILOGUE

"Peace of Mind Goes With Me"

Within
Lie the facets
We experience
Without

ACCEPT: Everyone as our teacher.

ultimate joining

FIND: *All* of the qualities we
attribute to others in
ourselves.

KNOW: The teachers are always
there.
The judgments fade.
Comparisons have less
reason.
The *need* to understand
diminishes.

And . . . for a moment . . . just a
moment . . . There is *no belief system*
. . . no B.S. There is *only*:

limitlessness   joining   stillness
peace   love   joy   listening
quiet   gentleness   now
and

When we return . . . and we will
to
Find ourselves in a belief system
we
See it as temporary . . .
Experience it as broader . . .
Feel less investment . . .
and

smile

Our sense of humor is still there
and
We know we are sane
and
So are the "others"

End of Scenario
Applaud Ourselves

Exuent

4 Stories About Labeling

When I think of my conscious mind as being the size of a keyhole and the rest of my awareness as being the size of the whole mansion, I then get some idea of the expansive awareness I am denying myself. This tool is at my disposal but it is rusting from lack of use and care. Why do I deny myself the use of this tool? It is because I choose to label my experience.

When we assign a *label* to someone or something we often relate to the label and not to the person or thing we have *labeled*. For example, we fill a box with goods to be stored in the garage, put a lid on the box, and label it. (Remember—the contents remain in the box even if your conscious mind "forgets" them.)

Now this process is very satisfying and tidy and a proper one for keeping things in order. Yet there's a problem: eventually we forget what is in the box. Moreover, boxes of more "stuff" are gradually added and soon the garage is full. It may take a major move to get us back into the garage to go through these boxes. When we eventually do, we discover treasures, junk, things we could have used had we remembered they were there, things we are sure we have never seen before in our lives, and some things that definitely don't belong in the "garage" category.

And so works our mind. *We* lose when we seal up our mental boxes. When we seal someone up and label them, we then relate to the label and not to the many rich dimensions of the person inside. *We lose.* We don't hurt *them* but as we see them in one dimension, that is usually all we allow them to experience of us; thus, we limit our interactions.

The following are some labeling practices I have observed, felt, and used. They have all impressed me deeply as examples of separation and fear, rather than joining and peace between fellow humans.

LABELING OTHERS

Most forms of labeling are upfront and can be detected quite easily. For example, suppose you see a rather unkempt person staggering toward you as they walk down the street. You *label* them as drunk, cross the street to avoid an uncomfortable encounter, and find out later that this person has a muscle coordination problem. The result is a missed opportunity to meet someone because of unfounded prejudice.

I had a great deal of fear that would well up in me every time I was around handicapped people. I excused my avoidance by telling myself I didn't want to patronize them or call attention to their handicap. I was also afraid that my emotions would overflow and I would gush tears, which would *really* be patronizing. So I just avoided them; I wouldn't even look at them or smile as I passed them on the streets (though I would do this for "normal" people). One of the most powerful experiences of my life occurred when I finally broke through my blockages and fears of approaching handicapped people.

A man confined to a wheel chair was attending a university where I was teaching. He was active in school and city politics and was responsible for much of the change in civic structures to accommodate the handicapped. I saw him almost every day and wanted very much to approach him as so many others did. While I admired them for talking to him, I hated the fearful part of me that held me back.

Finally my opportunity came. I saw him at an outdoor market selling his book. I walked past two or three times, my heart pounding, then I took the plunge. I could feel unwanted tears gushing to the surface. I decided that he had no doubt seen tears before and continued toward him. If I was to be a fool, with difficult-to-explain tears welling up, then so be it. Nothing would stop me this time.

I approached and kept coughing, like I had a ticklish throat that was making my eyes water. I said "Hi," and talked about how I'd seen him on campus and had always wanted to meet him. I heard myself prattling on about who I was and lots of other nervous chatter. I watched him come alive as I talked. His bottom seemed glued to the chair, but everything else was in motion. His arms twisted and turned, flailing out at odd angles. His bony knees sprung up. His head circled and with every other turn his eyes would get into position to see me. I squatted down. His mouth was open and drooling, teeth brown, crooked, rotten-looking. His tongue seemed to be in the way of his speech. When he spoke I could make out very little and had to ask for many repeats. We conversed for awhile, learning about each other. I wanted to touch him, like I would anyone else as I was getting acquainted. Would he be offended?

"May I give you a hug?" I asked.

The body motions accelerated. I jumped in when his head made a circle and his arms were open enough to receive my embrace. As we hugged, my tears became unmistakable sobs and I tried choking them back, something I have never done very well. I pulled away a little, keeping my hand on his knee—one of the fairly still parts of his body. His eyes were so warm and twinkly. I thought of how much I love being touched and wondered how much touching he gets. He's so full of loving energy. What does he do with it? Does he have someone to love who really loves him and doesn't pity him? Later, I read his book. It was about him and his lover and all of their traumas and joys, ecstasies and pain, anger and trust. It was about life, and it taught me so much.

OTHERS LABELING US

We have all experienced being labeled by "experts": "You can't sing, so mouth the words," or "The disease you have is incurable." We have also experienced the confusion of being labeled as something we do not identify with: "You must be a Christian," or "Obviously, you are too lazy to finish that job." All such labels cause some adverse reaction in us and they can even drastically alter our lives, if we choose to believe in or identify with them.

In my Yoga classes I regularly encounter people who are solving problems that their doctors said were impossible to overcome. John was in an auto accident and was put together piece-by-piece by skilled surgeons. He then spent years in physical therapy. He came to class, with some experience in Yoga gained before the accident, to seek gentle movement to gain increased strength and flexibility. His doctors are now taking X-rays to try and figure out how he is getting so much movement out of a body they had predicted would barely walk again.

I have always had a bit of a perverse streak and feel it rising with almost unbearable urgency when I feel someone tightening their category of definition about me. Sometimes I go along with them and even help them reinforce their judgment with some added evidence they haven't thought of yet. Other times I devilishly delight in recounting some of my more outlandish adventures, so I can watch their mental gears jam. After all, if the gears are jammed, maybe they won't be quite so ready to label again.

A woman approached me, after not seeing me in a year, and said, "I can see that you have made a complete change." My mind whirled . . . I thought, sure, I change every day, but what does she mean? I asked what she was referring to and she was incredulous that I would even ask. She mentioned my clothing as if it were an obvious indication of some deep philosophical shift. Mentally, I reviewed my clothing: skirt, blouse—nothing new in the last ten years! Then I remembered she had only seen me in my Yoga clothes in class and at retreats.

I was truly unable to continue the conversation because of the look on her face and in her eyes. Clearly, to her, I had slipped into some new category and now she was relating to me as being in this category. I watched with fascination as I witnessed this new perception influence her connection with me. I felt completely stopped. Should I defend myself, and if so, how? I decided to let it be, although, later I thought of some good ideas to share with her. At the time, however, I only felt a cold chill as I realized the power our appearance can have over our opinions about others.

MUTUAL LABELING

We often fall into habitual patterns or ways of relating to others that, as long as there is some pay-off, we continue to use, even though the pattern may result in pain. The following situation, described to me recently by a confused and unhappy person, illustrates such a pattern:

"When I come home my mate greets me with a barrage of things that have been neglected around the house: bills that need to be paid, accusations of not spending enough time with the children; a whole backlog of grievances— some related, some not. This is a pattern in our way of relating and I am tired of it. I'm tired of the nagging and the manner in which it is presented, but I can't seem to get out of it. I see my mate as constantly nagging and talking down to me. I don't even feel like coming home anymore. I hate the way we are relating; I hate the distance between us. Why can't she be grateful that I come home each day? I listen and usually end up doing everything just to get some peace, but inside I feel resentful and I can't see what the payoff is for me by participating in this rut."

The recognition of a pattern is a very important ingredient in learning to stop a cycle of unwanted interaction. But it is enough for now just to recognize a rut or habit. We will get into how to spring free of our self-made traps after a few more examples.

"GOOD" LABELS THAT DO NO GOOD

We know a bit about the problems of "putting people down," but have you considered the problems that can result from "putting people up"? An extremely common, yet subtle, form of separation occurs when we put people on pedestals. We may do this to admire and honor them, because we want a model or someone to follow, or we may want to believe someone is perfect—that there is someone someplace who knows what's happening, and can tell us how it is.

What is wrong with admiring and following someone who has good qualities to emulate? Nothing is wrong; it is simply a matter of learning to recognize our tendency to "pedestal-ize" someone, and then let go. We can learn to allow those we admire to inspire us to explore our own limitless potential using the energy they have stimulated in us. This is one of the beauties of performers. We can go to a performance and receive their gift of inspiration, but when the performance ends we have a choice: we can become a groupie or we can use the performer's gift as a valuable resource that can enrich our life.

Pedestals can be dramatic, like celebrity worship, or simple, everyday pedestals, like "my mate is perfect." In

either case separation is at work. With the pedestal label intact, we are relating to the label and *not* to the whole person.

The main problem with a pedestal is that it is such a long way down. My sensitivities have learned from long, hard experience that the trip to the top of the pedestal, no matter how soothing to the ego, is not worth the trip down. Also, when I put someone on a pedestal, where am I in relation to them? And besides, I get a kink in my neck from the strain of looking up. Whether I am on the pedestal or putting someone else on it, we are still separate from one another.

After realizing this, I watched myself put people on pedestals: after the first blush of flattery they seemed to squirm with the unrelenting focus and the responsibility it entailed. They didn't want to disappoint me by failing to live up to my expectations, but the effort left them feeling separate and miserable. They were unhappy with both the separation and the pressure to be perfect. They acted more like a butterfly specimen pinned through the middle, impaled for inspection, than the exalted figure I had showcased.

Putting others on a pedestal can also create problems for us. As long as we are dependent on others to lead us, we may find ourselves playing a secret game of resentment which is based on fear: fear that we don't have *it*, fear that we can't be perfect though someone else can. We are therefore not complete, and they are. If they don't give *it* to us we'll be without *it* and die! And if they leave we will be unwhole, incomplete. We begin to cater to the person we think has *it*, calling our attention "devotion" and "love," yet we are really holding them separate from us. We do not allow them to know our depths because they are special and we are not deserving. Thus, being admired is not the fulfillment of a fantasy as we might have thought.

My husband and I recently attended a performance of jugglers extraordinaire. They put on a magnificent show full of amazing feats and rich comedy. Watching them, I vacillated between complete awe at their skills and an absolute absorption and delight with their wit and spontaneity. I left feeling that the things I am juggling in my life were a little lighter. And having witnessed feats that some corner of my mind says couldn't be done, I felt a little daylight had been shed into my own limited corners. I felt good and light, a little clearer, and more daring as I thanked and blessed them for their generous gift of lightness.

LABELING OURSELVES

We do one of our heaviest labeling jobs on ourselves. Most of this labeling happens on less conscious levels; often, it is based on an assumption acquired long ago which still remains in our less-conscious awareness, in the form of a belief system. Most such labeling is the result of *comparing* ourselves to others, and then *categorizing* ourselves. For example, we may say to ourselves: "I'm not as pretty as Jane is, so I must be unattractive." In the next five sections I will illustrate how we build imaginary fences around ourselves; how we limit our creativity and self-expression by affixing labels to ourselves and then passively accepting them as fact.

Labeling Our Capabilities

I taught music for twenty-five years. During that time, I estimate that over 300 people, mostly men, have told me they don't sing because as a child an adult told them they couldn't sing on pitch. They proved this advice correct by no longer practicing. Craig is a classic example of this phenomena. He came into our professional singing group as an accompanist. At the time, we also needed a tenor, but he said he couldn't sing on pitch. I asked him if anything was wrong with his hearing—he said no. His speaking voice had a nice tenor quality and a ring to it that I knew would produce a good singing tone. At first he panicked at the prospect of singing, but then he went to work, trusting in and relying on the faith I had in him until he could find it on his own. Three years later, he was teaching a voice class at a community college.

A little girl has tried for several years to convince me that she is stupid and bad . . . because that's how she feels about herself. She keeps showing me with example after example. I am not convinced and she has just about run out of things to do, although there *are* still a few things she hasn't tried. I keep telling her that I'm not particularly fond of her behavior at times, but I also keep reminding her that I love her and feel that she is a very sensitive, good person. I feel her giving in a little; just recently, the drama quieted a fraction—where she used to scream and break things, she now just pouts and stomps out of the room. This is a sign that she is through testing me and my opinion of her, and is beginning the terribly scary process of believing herself to be capable, valuable, and lovable. Although she will have relapses, they will be like gentle winds compared to the previous typhoon.

I feel she is on her way. She is starting the painful process of switching her labels. It *can* be a painful process to change from a "bad" label to a "good" one. Any change requires adjustment, not only on her part, but on the part of all the people in her life.

Labeling Ourselves as Perfect Mates and Parents

Another self-label is the *label of perfect mates and parents*. The perfect wife and mother keeps an immaculate house, cooks gourmet meals, works part-time or volunteers, sends the children to the best schools, and is too busy to make love with her husband or to cuddle with the children over a story. The perfect husband and father works two jobs to make lots of money to provide for his family all the things the ads say they need to make them happy, and has no time to make love with his wife or cuddle with the children over a game. How do the children *label* this when they are twenty-five-years old? What have they learned about being mates and parents?

We Label Past Wrongs: Blaming Ourselves and Others

Many times we do not know of labels we may be carrying in our subconscious until we make plans. By setting a goal to improve a situation and then observing how we fail to follow through with it, we can learn a great deal about our hidden programming. For example, if my hidden belief is that I am "bad," then I don't deserve "good" things happening to me. I have received many calls from "well"-intentioned people who plan to take my class. Later, when they don't follow through, I find myself wondering what sidetracked them this time.

Is the following dialogue familiar to you? "This year I wanted to sign up for Yoga class so that my body/mind would feel more coordinated and flexible. I called the teacher and got all of the details . . . but I never went. Why am I not doing what I say I want to do? It must be my mother's fault . . . she didn't set a good example. Or maybe it's my mate's fault . . . no encouragement. Once it was bad luck . . . the one class I went to was cancelled, and once it was my body's fault—I had a cold. All these things are holding me back, I really want to go . . . *It isn't my fault!!!*"

This is where the thinking seems to lead when we indulge in accepting status as a victim. Though we may think we are progressing by identifying bigger and better targets for our blame, this is not the case; we are simply stuck. We become "victims" when we believe that something or someone has the power to make or break us. Conversely, when we believe that we have the power to make or break someone else we are still a "victim" of the same power game in reverse. It doesn't matter which end of the pedestal we are on, it is still separation and we still lose.

This thinking is based on the assumption that someone must be in or out of power rather than assuming that everyone can be empowered. As I feel a sense of my own power, I also empower you, and as I empower you I feel a sense of my own power. It is not a teeter-totter. We don't have to have one up and one down. With mutual effort, we both can be up like a well-balanced lift.

We Label Our Mistakes and Accidents as Chance Happenings

It is so easy to dismiss an event as luck, as something we have no control over, or as something to fix up and get into running order. When we open to the possibility of sharing the responsibility for minor or major events in our lives we have taken an important step toward gaining more power over our lives and getting along better with others. The example that follows might have been overlooked at another time in my life, but in fact it was a great teacher for me. The lesson was subtle and could easily have been ignored; after all, much in our culture seems to reinforce the desire to get attention as a victim.

After twenty-five years of driving with only one slight bump, I had a strong premonition that I would be involved in an auto accident. I meditated and asked for inner guidance about the lesson I needed from an auto wreck. What was it I needed to learn that would take something as drastic as a wreck to teach me? I wanted to skip the actual wreck and still learn what I needed to learn from the experience. Nothing came forth except a dream of having an accident. I decided that I had gotten my lesson, though I wasn't sure what the lesson was.

A month later someone hit my car . . . I was not even in it. A real accident and not my *fault*. How could it possibly be? No lesson for *me* here . . . maybe it was for the guy who had no insurance but paid me anyway. Of course, I experienced a little lost time getting the car to the shop, and met some nice people in the process. Premonition and lesson must be fulfilled.

Three months later I had my second accident. Someone hit the side of my car. He was drunk, and had cut in from a side road and hit my fender. He contested my claim a little, but even his own insurance company said it was obviously his *fault*. The car was okay and again I was blameless, though again, I lost a little time with repairs. Pleasant people helped me and I even had money left over from what the insurance paid. By now, my concern was growing: another wreck and this time I was in the car! The lesson was becoming clearer: I was seeing myself as a victim, feeling victimized someplace in my life. I knew I had to let go of playing this role, so I took a closer look and acknowledged the places I was playing victim. I recognized I'd been carrying around more of this energy than I thought. I released it all. I threw it off the "Bridge of Release." I gave it to the universe. I vowed to forgive myself and the people I felt had wronged me. So, now I was really finished with the wreck I had envisioned . . . I had finally gotten the lesson! I felt elated!

Three months later—third wreck. Someone hit my car. This time I was in another city and I had a passenger in the car, as well. Clearly, the wrecks were getting more complex. But the car was okay, the insurance was paid. I could continue. Where was the lesson? I was frightened and wanted help. I took a closer look and asked for more clarity; *something* was missing. I was about to start a 7,000 mile trip by myself and I didn't want to play dodge-em all the way. Three wrecks . . . Help! I was really listening now! And sure enough, a lesson came through in my meditation that felt solid . . . with unmistakable ease and peaceful knowing:

> There is no perfection . . . no ultimate state where all is "right" . . . no happily ever after . . . I will never totally let my victim memories go. So—I must simply accept myself as I am, with all my faults. My failings are my teacher; they help me to remain compassionate with others.

This message was telling me that there is no end to my feelings of being victimized. There is no perfect state on this earth where I will never again feel like a victim; no guarantee that whenever some unpleasant event occurs, I will not be engulfed by a strong feeling of being a victim. And this is a blessing, not a curse, as it helps me to stay compassionate. The difference is that now I feel victimized for *seconds* as compared to *years* before. I no longer seriously accept the concept of being victimized. I now know I have a choice in the way I behave.

As I let go of participating in life as a victim, I was able to open to broader insights and understandings. By dropping the label "accident," and viewing events as "teachings," I was able to learn a profound lesson about how I was conducting my life. As I took more responsibility, I felt more free and safe in the world.

Labeling Our Sensitivities

Not all the pain, discomfort, and confusion we feel are our own. You have most likely experienced a rush of happiness when a really joyful person has come in with hugs and gifts and a zest for life pouring out of them. Their joy seems infectious. It is, and we *are* uplifted by their presence. The opposite is also familiar: a relative may come home with a cold, tired and cynical after a hard day, and the whole house takes on an aura of gloom.

Whatever someone else is feeling and experiencing, on some level we are sharing that feeling and experience with them. Of course, we will believe it is our feeling and interpret it according to our own fears, as in the following example: A man comes home to find his wife a bit distant and quiet. She has just broken a favorite and expensive vase he had given her and feels guilty and careless and doesn't want to talk about it yet. Because he is feeling insecure about her affection, he takes the quiet to mean something is wrong in their relationship. He also doesn't want to talk about it now. They go through their evening with politeness and courtesy, each nurturing their private thoughts and experiencing their separate fears.

I suspect we may have several hundred senses rather than five or six, if we could classify them all. We are super-sensitive creatures with finely tuned antennae; we simply have problems interpreting the data we receive. I feel that our sensitivities pick up subtle waves of energy from others all the time, and it is difficult to separate their feeling from our own.

We are an outer-oriented society. The presence of mammoth "beauty" industries—makeup manufacturers, the fashion industry, cosmetic surgeons and related "makeover" technologies—proves the truth of this statement. Outwardly, we may be fooled by what we see consciously, while our less-conscious awareness is monitoring the true message. Consider, for example, the "jovial fat person" that we *see* and the "bruised inner person" that we *feel*. Is it any wonder that we walk away from this "jovial" person feeling tired? Our less-conscious awareness knows the truth if we can only learn to listen to it.

I offer the following stories to illustrate how this can happen: Beverly called to ask if we could talk after class. As we sat together she started chatting a bit obliquely. I was glad she was wandering for the moment because I was having difficulty concentrating. Waves of fear were moving through my body. My mind was racing from concern for my three-year-old, to worries connected with my divorce, to my two older sons. Twenty other thoughts, all revolving around fear, darted through my mind as I tried to listen to her. Finally, I broke the momentum by saying "Beverly, are you afraid of something?" She burst into tears and then what she wanted to share came tumbling out and my feelings about the still-undefined fear vanished. Only then could I give her the attention and comfort she needed. I had been feeling her fear and assuming it was my own, though it was not my feeling until I adopted it and translated it into what would provoke fear for me.

About that same time, a Yoga student told me of a pain she was experiencing in her back. She asked if I would keep her in mind during class and let her know which postures might not be good for her. I agreed and started class. Soon I became aware of a pain in my lower back, in an unfamiliar place for my body to feel pain. I continued class, and found it quite easy to keep the woman in mind because of this coincidence of having pain where she had it. I mentioned movements here and there that might not be good for her. After class she thanked me for the personal attention and said that her back felt better and that she was glad she had come. As I packed up and walked out I realized that my pain had also disappeared.

This was the first time I was consciously aware of literally taking on another's pain. I felt grateful for the teaching imparted by the pain, especially in such a large class (there were forty students), and also appreciated that it wasn't my pain to keep. This type of situation became common once I recognized the sudden appearance of similar symptoms. I no longer feared this pain, but simply asked the pain if it was mine, as I had done with Beverly's fear. If it was mine it stayed and if it was another's it left immediately with just a thought. As soon as its message had been clearly delivered and received, it miraculously vanished.

Here are some practices that can help us with the floating energy we pick up in the bank line or on the streets or from closer contacts with others.

First, accept that the feelings you are experiencing are real and that you have a choice about how much to allow into your being.

Second, make it a high priority to get to know yourself as thoroughly and honestly as you can so that you can more easily distinguish between your feelings and responses and those of someone else. Most people are like a window clouded with dust and rubble; they have been collecting "stuff" from birth, and maybe before. Cleaning the window helps and a program of regular maintenance will keep it clean.

Third, use some regularly practiced process such as the "Bridge of Release" or the "Leaf in the Water" (described in Chapter Six). These practices will help you to shed old ways of thinking and of being in the world that no longer seem to fit.

Fourth, practice having an invisible, see-through shield around you. You can interact as much as you want, and the other person's energy remains with them. Or, see yourself as being like a screen. Everything can pass through you without stopping or having any effect on you. Our personalities and moods differ and any of these practices can be helpful, if you use them.

5 | Labeling

Perhaps my stories of labeling, comparing, judging, categorizing, and blaming resonated with some of your experiences. As I reflected on these and many other experiences I'd had, I realized how much my belief systems and attitudes toward life were invested in the ongoing process of labeling the people, things, and events in my life. I seemed to feel a satisfaction in categorizing. It was as if some part of me thought that if I categorized someone, they would stay put and I could then move freely. If I could label someone I would no longer have to consider them an individual; thus, it would be easier to divide the world into "us" and "them" without having to answer to any bothersome moral questions.

As I looked back at the ways I had invested in my labels and manipulated to make them work, I felt a personal dishonesty and uneasiness. It seemed I was stuck with some unproductive habits I was still reluctant to give up. My future plans were colored by my expectation of goals to be accomplished and the fear of failing to achieve them.

I wanted freedom from my emotional, mental, physical, and spiritual pain. I found a large portion of this pain was caused by my habit of labeling because this led to separation from others. Because many of these practices were habitual and subconscious, I felt I had to first uncover the patterns that produced these labels.

To learn more about my less-conscious motivation, I began to examine the processes I was using to get what I wanted in life. Up to this time I had believed things occurred happily sometimes and unhappily at other times. I had overlooked the role my intention played in leading up to the event. Now I had taken a huge step—I was willing to look at this part I was playing in setting up the process.

INVESTING IN LABELS

Each of our actions can affect the entire world. Taking full responsibility for what happens in life may seem beyond our abilities, but in fact, it allows us to recognize our power. If we can take the time to understand what we might be gaining from our present situation, we can often find another way to obtain what we want—a way which is more positive for our total health. Our failure to take responsibility for the things that happen to us may well be due to the payoff we receive when we invest in labels. It is obvious that we are receiving *some* sort of payoff with a label, or we wouldn't continue with it. If we accept that, it will be easier to determine the nature of our payoff.

There was a time in my life when I was frequently ill, so I decided to observe these incidents more closely to see what benefits I was receiving from being sick. Some payoffs were quite obvious: I got special attention, I didn't have to feel guilty about being served, I had an acceptable excuse to let go of my duties, I was not blamed for not accomplishing, and I was able to avoid doing what I didn't want to do or was afraid to do with good grace.

However, these were merely superficial benefits; as it turned out, the real payoff was happening on a deeper level of my being. I realized that I couldn't receive support, caring, or concern from others with a clear conscience. I looked at how I accepted the generosity and kindness of others in my everyday life and found that I was clearly more of a giver than a receiver. Being ill allowed me to temporarily accept the goodwill of others without guilt, without feeling that I was "losing control."

We get away with this because in our society a giver is admired, even respected, though most of us overlook the fact that a giver is also in control. When giving, I am in an active mode, in charge; when receiving I am passive, waiting for something to happen to me. My conscious mind wants to be in control and my less-conscious awareness plans ways for me to surrender. Thus, to maintain some balance in my life, I get ill in order to give up my control and allow the receptive state to dominate for awhile.

My illnesses are one example of a *label* I applied to myself (a "victim" of repeated illnesses) which I chose to *invest* in (by refusing to question the presence of these illnesses in my life, or to ask myself what the payoff might have been). Before I made the conscious decision to fully understand either the label or the illnesses, the idea of letting go of the "victim" label was threatening. My decision to carefully explore the situation, however, was in fact an act of taking responsibility for my well-being. Once I had done this, I gained a great deal of *power* over my life: I was no longer a passive victim (goodbye, label), but an active force in the outcome of every aspect of my life.

Once we realize we have this power, we can apply it where it will be most beneficial for us. If we continue to refuse the responsibility of owning our power, we remain semi-directionless, always a helpless victim, with no control over our life.

At what expense to ourselves do we continue our labeling practices? What is the price we pay by not listening to our body, mind, emotions, and intuitive messages? Clearly, as we label, we limit ourselves and others. It is as if we are puppies who have been raised in cages. When the door is opened we shrink back in the cage, trembling in fear of the unknown. We have to be coaxed out with guidance and an understanding hand. And this new territory, though free, is not without its pitfalls: we could be hit by a car or beaten or starved. But is our only choice to live in fear and trembling, safely locked in our familiar cage? It is only an illusion of safety; a fire or flood could turn the cage into a death trap. And to live only in a cage will limit our life, stunt our growth. What price do we pay to avoid risks in our lives and relationships?

Another less obvious problem in labeling is that we even separate "ourselves" from "our bodies." It is as if our body was attacking us and making us sick. Unfortunately, we often do with parts of our body what we do with people who bother us—get rid of them.

Intense pain can be the result of feeling separate from others and from our bodies. If we feel that our body is getting ill and we have no say in the matter, then we may soon feel attacked by our body . . . a *victim* of our *own* body! This is denying that the mind has any control over the body—it perpetuates the believe that mind/body/spirit are separate. Separation is confusion and pain. In joining mind/body/spirit, we befriend our whole system as one entity. And if any part of that whole system shows symptoms of distress, we can address the whole system for healing.

Labeling is a complicated subject. As I studied its effect on my relationships, I began to perceive many diverse forms and found myself exploring ever more subtle areas of my less-conscious behavior.

One of the interesting things I found is that we often label something for convenience in the moment and then start treating the label as solid fact. The label gets mixed in with other information we may have gathered more carefully, yet we act on it all the same. For example, I see a woman with long hair and immediately think, "Oh, she's a hippie." This label is a casual judgment made purely on the basis of a single characteristic. The next time I see this woman, however, she is "that hippie" and suddenly the label connotes all the negative associations involved with being a hippie—dirty, into drugs, spaced-out, and so on. If this woman were ever to apply for a position over which I had some authority, my concept of her would, no doubt, prompt me to deem her unsuitable for the position. Thus, in labeling others, we start on a shaky foundation, yet we expect to erect a sound building.

We truly underestimate the complexity of our minds. I think we are aware of our cognitive powers; what we underestimate is that part of our mind that selects the "items for recall." Our wonderful mental capacity opens to and selects the information that we *want* to be aware of, according to our programming and intention. In our desire to accomplish some goal, we may overlook important evidence that suggests this goal is not the best to pursue. It is at this point that taking full responsibility for every event in our lives will help us to move beyond the confines of "seeing only what we want to see" and into the realm of "seeing what we need to see" for the benefit of our full being.

Unless we can discover the subconscious obstacles we create to avoid taking responsibility we will continue to limp along, patching up problems here and there, until we tire of repairing the same spots over and over. Our desire to be right is one of the most devious tricks our ego plays. As long as we fall for it we will stay in our self-made rut until we tire of the game and *really* want out.

By learning to be truly responsible for whatever is going on, I feel we *can* easily know clearly what we want, beyond our superficial desires, because we have opened to a *new way* of evaluating existing data.

If we ask enough for the ability to take full responsibility for our life, we will get it. It may not come in the form we expect, but it will come. Often the gift of renewal will come through a cataclysmic change in our lives like an illness or injury, the death or loss of a loved one, an unexpected inheritance, or a job change.

HOW WE USE LABELS

Relationship dynamics are wonderfully complex and provide an excellent backdrop for examining how we use labels. Here are a few ways that we use roles to keep our partners separate from us:

Blaming makes a division of me = right—you = wrong.
Other roles can be:

me = victim	you = bully
me = abused	you = abuser
me = prey	you = hunter
me = underdog	you = top dog
me = deserted	you = deserter

In all cases the duration of these roles depends on the willingness of both partners to continue to use them. At any time, either partner may declare a desire to change roles; when this happens the other must also change or leave the game. If you are afraid to change roles because you feel that the consequences will be too severe, then you must accept that you are staying in that role by choice. When you decide to face the consequences, whatever they might be, then you have made a choice to change your role.

I once was playing the victim role and felt very frightened by the "bully," until one day I stood firm at the top of the stairs. As he came rushing up the stairs toward me, full of anger, I felt calm and strong in my decision not to turn and run. When he arrived at the top of the stairs, we just stood there for a moment, recognizing that somehow a role had been changed, and the other must now change too. A pattern of relating had been broken and amid its ruins lay the opportunity for growth.

In any relationship either person may switch roles or leave the game at any time. It is only when we think we have no choice that we find ourselves stuck in an undesirable role—but we *do* always have a choice. We can always choose again if we have taken a path that has become unsuitable.

Sometimes a partner is so reluctant to give up a role that it takes the threat of leaving to break through this reluctance. And this might be a good time to try and reach a compromise and enter into a dialogue to help resolve the conflict. The bully may not *want* to remain a bully, but holds on because he or she knows no other way and is afraid. When the victim tires of the role and threatens to leave, the bully feels even *greater* fear, but there is also an opportunity to explore other ways of relating that are more compatible with the former victim's newly emerging identity.

Relationships are shifting and changing constantly. We play variations and take up many roles almost daily. The more obvious exterior role may mask suppressed inner roles that we are also playing. When a person appears to be a heavy victim, I have learned to look deeper to find where the tyrant lurks. Though some roles seem to take precedence, we only emphasize, for our own game plan, certain facets of our being at any one time.

We can learn more about ourselves by letting others be our mirror. In my relationship with my husband, for example, I have learned that what I see in him usually manifests as the opposite in me: if my critic is working overtime and I see him as being too pushy, I have learned to look to myself to see why I want to be pushed around. Maybe I'm feeling tired and want to turn the management reins over to him for a little while; thus, if I appear weak and ineffective he will have to take more responsibility. By this subtle role I am encouraging the very assertiveness I am complaining about.

We often complain most bitterly about an action or trait in someone else at about the time we are ready to change or cycle out of that trait in ourselves.As we reach this higher level of awareness, we are often amazed to realize that by making a change, we can induce the desired change in our partner as well. My way out of feeling pushed around by my husband is to observe the way I am viewing him. If

I am seeing him as "pushy," then I ask myself what a "pushy" person would need in a partner. The answer is: a pushy person needs someone who wants to be pushed around. Thus, I don't have to change him; I simply need to decide whether I am content with my role of being pushed around in this partnership.

This is where relationships frequently break down: we label, judge, and rank our partners and then try to change them to suit our judgment of how we think they *should* be. When we are content with judging and solving what's wrong with *them*, we no longer stop to worry about it, but we have missed the point entirely. When we are only concerned with changing our partner, we fail to examine our role in the partnership; thus, we miss the opportunity to change the behavior patterns we don't like in ourselves.

The teaching value in defining my role is that once I discover what my role is, I can take back the power I have given away. When I take responsibility for accepting my label, or the role I am playing, rather than blame parents, teachers, or other frequently used scapegoats, I can reclaim the power I have wasted in reinforcing the label. When I appreciate all the hard work and skill it takes to create and carry out my role, I then can appreciate my perseverance, ingenuity, and cleverness, and use this newly found power and energy in more productive ways in my life.

WHEN WE LABEL, WE:

- Only see the dimensions that we have labeled (denying the rest) and therefore limit the relationship,
- Continue searching outside of ourselves for satisfaction, finding new candidates who only disappoint us when they fail to live up to our expectations, and
- Build our anger and resentment toward what we think are "superficial" people.

Thus, because we have labeled our world, it is just as we suspected: our negative expectations and predictions of never finding a rich and fulfilling relationship come true. We prove ourselves "right." The others out there are no good and it's *no fault of mine.*

We find ourselves *stuck.* And we will remain stuck here until the gift of pain in some form—mental, emotional, physical, or spiritual—becomes so great that we let go of our investment in being right and seek another way.

So, we can ask ourselves: "Would I rather be right or be happy and feel peaceful?" What can we do? We can look at *everyone and everything* in our lives as our teachers, listen to the people and events we are excluding from our lives. Our teachers are with us in all ways, always.

LOCKED IN THE TRAP OF LABELING

The following is a summary of how we label our experiences and the results of this labeling:

- We *label* someone or something because of what we know, from past experience.
- We *invest* in this *label* and *control* or *manipulate* people or events to make it work.
- We disregard *evidence* that shows the label is inappropriate, dismissing it as *accidents* or *mistakes.*
- The result becomes a *pattern* that we trust and a *future goal* is set using the trusted *plan.*
- We *expect* perfection and happiness at *completion.*
- If our *expectations* are not fulfilled, we *blame* the guilty "others" who *caused* the failure, try to change their thinking, or get rid of them so we can be *right.*

Does this sound like any relationships you know?
Now, what is wrong with this familiar pattern of logical

thinking? Everyone needs a plan! When a building falls down do we check to see what was wrong on the top floor or do we examine the foundation first? Here we go back to the foundation of the whole plan . . . the *label* we start with.

In my story in the previous chapter about the car wrecks, I could have easily and justifiably rested my case with bad luck, or strange stars in the sky, and I would have gotten plenty of peer support for my label: "Poor me, a victim of circumstances beyond my control. How could I possibly be to blame? In one case I wasn't even in the car!"

Blame is one of the labels we most commonly use when we want to stop thinking about a problem. We play the narrow game of placing blame in order to attain the dubious satisfaction of relieving ourselves of responsibility. And, by adding to the belief that others will try to hurt us, we reinforce our fears of being the "victim."

Only when we stop *blaming* will we have the opportunity to open to other interpretations of events. There is a reason why a woman "accidentally" marries three abusive mates in a row, though she may blame "bad luck." If she can recognize her responsibility in the selection process, she has a chance to move beyond a very destructive pattern of getting someone to punish her for whatever she feels she has done wrong. When she forgives herself she will be able to marry someone who respects her as much as she has learned to respect herself.

Look into your life for repeated patterns, such as my car wrecks or the woman's three abusive husbands. The ruts you are in may want to teach you something before you can leave them.

Most often we do not examine events or people for similarities, but instead fool ourselves with differences. We think we have something new in front of us because its appearance is different: the new lover does not resemble the old one, the car is a different make, the new boss is paying me more, and so on.

TOOLS FOR MOVING BEYOND LABELS

One method I used for learning about myself was to lis- ten to my words and thoughts toward myself and others throughout the day. What we say is our first great clue to what is happening inside. I found two tools particularly helpful: listening to my words, using a tape recorder; and a day of silence to listen to my thoughts.

With the tape recorder I taped myself for thirty minutes as I talked about my life, relationships, neighbors, likes and dislikes, work, and so on. Then I listened to myself with a very critical ear for words that devalued others, thoughts that cancelled out what I thought I wanted, tones that sounded hopeless or had a helpless, whining timbre, and anything else that sounded defeated and lacked joy. What I heard were the words and thoughts that I had pro- grammed myself with day after day. I listened and learned and wept over what I heard and cringed at the thought of others hearing "poor me" for so many years.

There is much to be said about the "hows" and "whys" of listening to yourself. I urge you to try it by taping yourself and *listening to it.* You will get the messages that you want to hear at this time. If we can accept that we are program- ming ourselves with every thought and word, then at some point it will become very important to clean up our input. After all, what we program ourselves with is what we will act on, and we *are* in charge of the programming.

At the time I decided to do a day of silence I was work- ing as a music specialist for a grade school. For years I had laryngitis every three months. The pattern of such a regular occurrence eventually filtered through to my con- scious awareness. I decided to have a day of silence before getting an attack of laryngitis, to see if that might have any effect. It worked! I realized my body had been telling me I needed to rest or at least be quiet approximately every three months. I usually continued teaching and enjoyed the students' responses to my silence. They were quieter and some whispered to me in sympathetic response. A day of silence can be easily arranged if you want it enough.

Whenever I enjoyed a day of silence I listened to my thoughts about everyone and everything. I heard my judgments, criticisms, and the things I "almost" said. I noticed that the times I normally used my voice to control a situation were the times when it was hardest to remain silent. I was particularly impressed, or I should say depressed, with how I used my voice with my children. Because, in silence, I needed to go to them and touch them to get their attention, I realized I was controlling them at a distance with my voice. While I was silent, they responded more gently and I felt the bond I'd been missing by keeping my distance from them with my voice.

Some people balk at a day of silence, feeling it is too hard to do at work or with their families. Pretend to have laryngitis for a day if you don't want to tell people you are experiencing a day of silence. Your silence is an adjustment for others; their response can be less than reinforcing because your silence can cause them discomfort. It is a perfect example of how even a slight change in one partner can demand a dramatic shift in the other.

Remember that while a day of silence when you are alone is powerful, a day of silence in the presence of family and co-workers can be profound.

After using these tools to examine our tendencies to label, we can decide what action is to be taken, if any. If our labeling makes us unhappy, then perhaps it is time to make a shift in the way we categorize ourselves and our world. Before we can discard a pattern or even alter it we need to understand and accept the purpose for which we created it in the first place. If we don't recognize that we are creating our options, we will not be able to find the cause of our confusion and pain. When we accept our power and its role in creating our difficulties, at least we know *we* did it. The next step is to learn how to love ourselves regardless of the mess we may have created, and to appreciate that at one time we had a good reason for acting as we did. Then we can channel the same powerful energy into creating something more suitable for the present. If we don't acknowledge responsibility for our problems and continue to blame others, we will never comprehend that we can make things work ourselves.

If you have chosen after reading this far to let go of some of the labeling practices you may be participating in, here is a six-step process that will help you shed some of these.

1. Recognize how you are labeling.
   "Members of the opposite sex will hurt me."

2. Discover how that label has been of use up to now.
   "It keeps the opposite sex at a distance while I grow up, and get to know myself" or "It keeps me from bearing children and complicating my life."

3. Decide if you *truly* want to give up the label.
   "I'm ready now, but I am scared. I've believed in that label for so many years."

4. Get your intention clearly focused.
   "I want a beautifully fulfilling relationship with the opposite sex. I am ready for a relationship now that I know myself better."

5. Set a plan of action in motion that suits the situation.
   "I will make affirmations and set in motion some active seeking." "I have a deeply fulfilling relationship with someone special." "I deserve a loving relationship in my life now." "I plan to go to a workshop on intimate friendships and soulmates in two weeks to meet like-minded people."

6. Let it be all right whether you rid yourself of the labeling practice immediately or in a few years.
   "If I don't get instantaneous success, that is okay. It may take me a little more time than I think to truly rid myself of the effects of living with my label for so long."

Healing is in the instant. . . . Repair may take longer.

We will label something as long as it serves our purposes, though it may not be clear *what* the payoff is or *how* it is serving us. When my intention is clear, I will experience evidence that I am free of using a particular label. If success is not evident, I look for lack of clarity in my intention (Step 4). Be patient and resist *labeling* yourself "unsuccessful" if you don't get results right away. Stay with Step 2 until you realize how the label may still be serving you. Most times the demarcation point is not clear, but at some point down the road you will realize that you haven't used the label you are trying to discard for a long time.

Here is an example of how I used this process to let go of a most embarrassing label. An overweight psychic who I had just met at a dinner explained that some people have a great deal of difficulty being around fat people. No conversation had lead up to his statement.

I froze. "He's reading my mind!" I had been sitting through the entire meal not being able to think of anything but his fat. I had one judgment after another: "If he's so psychic, why doesn't he lose weight?" "Here's another guru-type preaching veggies and clean living while porking out himself," and on and on.

I really took a look at my mind in that painful moment, knowing that my mind had been about ten percent on my dinner conversation and the rest on fat and my critical judgments. I realized that I had a real preoccupation with fat; this had never occurred to me before. I had opened to Step 1 of the process of recognizing the label I had been using. I also made a quick mental survey and found that I had no friends who were fat. This was also a new realization. I kept searching my heart to see why I had such a prejudice and fear of fat. I wasn't fat, I hadn't been frightened by a fat person; maybe I was fat in a past life . . . so my mind went, searching and not finding anything to *blame.* Anyway, the past didn't really matter because I was experiencing my prejudice *now.* What was I going to do about it?

I moved to Step 5 by deciding to seek out and befriend

fat people to see what would happen. I gave myself a week to show some action on my resolve. At week's end there was no action and lots of excuses, including: "No fat people to be found." "No time." "No opportunity." "Today, I met one person who was slightly round." I tried another week and still no results. I began to suspect that I was sabotaging my own plan. I asked myself, "Why?"

I went back to Step 2 and searched my heart for how this label was serving me. What was I avoiding? . . . or more clearly, what did I fear? I had no clear answers and moved into another week with firm resolve and a specific target—Eileen. Eileen was a neighbor who was also a perfect candidate; she was overweight, and somehow in two years I had never managed more than a brief hello when I saw her outside. The week went by with no move on my part, though there were lots of excuses: the kids were sick, it was raining, I had a headache, and so on.

Back to Step 2 once more as I asked myself, "What am I afraid of?" I knew that if it was something I really wanted to do I would have already done it. I was not afraid of Eileen . . . well, I did fear that she would sense my bad feelings toward her fat—that must be it! As the weeks rolled by I watched my avoidance (avoid-dance), until I was really tired of my game. I considered giving up the project entirely, thinking, "This is dumb."

Instead, I chose to dig deeper, determined to get past this block to my awareness. My determination was fueled by my annoyance with myself for thwarting my own efforts. Part of me really wanted to hold on to what was familiar, but an even stronger part of me wanted to let go of anything that was blocking my full understanding. I felt at war inside.

I wanted to understand why I have excluded fat people from my life. I stayed with it through tears and impatience until I got an answer that felt like I had budged the block. The answer that finally came said, "I am terrified of getting fat myself. If I keep thinking of fat as revolting then I will avoid it and stay with a slimming diet out of fear of being thought revolting." When I connected to this, the tears of recognition came and I felt soft, compassionate, caring, loving feelings for myself and for all those, fat and thin, who may be experiencing a similar consciousness. I marvelled at what a complicated path I had set for myself. It seemed far easier to simply discipline myself to stick to a proper diet, than to reject a whole group of people who happened to be fat.

This story does not have the usual "happy ending." Eileen and I did not become bosom buddies. I *did*, however, get the message and this connection with a significant inner awareness *was* important. There came a time when I did feel ready to relate to the "person" Eileen rather than the "research project" named Eileen. A few months later I realized that I had a fat person for a friend through my work. It didn't even occur to me to think of her as "fat," though, until our third meeting. When I saw that my prejudice had been diffused, I felt joy and pleasure in the fact that I had worked to release that label so completely. Now I could enjoy my new friend for her full personality and not be distracted by my reaction to her fat.

COMING OF AGE—THE RITES OF TAKING RESPONSIBILITY

I admire other cultures that have clearly defined traditional rituals that note and honor points of passage in peoples' lives. I feel we lack this advantage in our American melting pot. However, it has occurred to me that I and others I have met and counseled have our particular "Modern-Day-Coming-of-Age-Rite." This rite occurs when we put away the need to follow, and honor our entry into fully responsible adulthood. A special "Coming-of-Age" occurs when we let go of outside influences and make our decisions based on inner guidance from our less-conscious awareness.

For me, the coming-of-age rite occurred as I became fully responsible, quit the victim/bully game, and learned to honor all of life's events as teachers and helpers. This was a time when I made a stand to assert what was right for me, taking into account my individuality, my purpose in life, and my personal standards. It was a time to open to another way of being, no less scary than an Indian youth's lone journey to gain entry into full adulthood.

When I felt sufficiently comfortable with this mode of operation in my life, I honored myself and my rite-of-passage with a ceremony which my friends attended as my witnesses. I continue to use this ritual for those I work with when we both feel that they have cleansed themselves enough of their habitual ruts to recognize ineffective patterns in time to avoid acting on them. When they can stop their thoughts and actions long enough to reach for the proper tool from their inner guidance they are ready to acknowledge themselves as an example for their world to emulate. They are teachers "by example" who have crossed over a very adult threshold, and they deserve a ceremony to announce this. The ceremony can be as simple as meditating on a mountaintop, to holding an elaborate party.

Today there is far less support from peers than Indian adolescents had when going on their vision quests. If what has been said here speaks to you at this time, then let this book be the peer support you need for your individual journey to self-recognition, appreciation, acceptance, respect, and love. Acknowledge that all there is lies within us, ready to teach us all we need to know. It's readily available and free of charge.

> The spacious deep
>   becomes the setting
>   for white jewels
>   of unexplored regions.
>
> Dark blue reaches
>   touch the sparkling dots
>   of endless reminder.
>
> Pinpricks of light pierce the dark
>   and touch
>   the memory of my soul.

All is within view
    no secret doors
        mysterious passageways
            or special keys.

Tomorrow's journey
    is ready today . . .
        you've but to turn to it
            and smile . . .

There's no place to go, it is here, just open to it. I wrote this poem at the time of my own transition. My own "Rite of Passage" was taking place . . . and no one was there to acknowledge it and celebrate with me. No one even seemed to understand what I was saying. It was frustrating and a little frightening when the one person who I thought *had* understood told me that they didn't have the slightest idea of the meaning of my poems. At least I thought I had a little company for awhile. I vowed then to be available for others as they take their first tentative steps into the lesser-known parts of their consciousness.

It can be a frightening commitment to make that first step. After that it is a continual unfoldment of pure joy and peace.

6 | Meditation

Meditation is the key to embracing the concepts discussed in this book. It is also a maintenance program for keeping sane. It takes us past our conscious mind-cgo-attached-competitive-separate self into the Self that on some level is joined with all others. Meditation can help us find a oneness with all humanity while giving us the clarity to nurture our individuality.

I am overwhelmed when I look back on my life and see how often I have *chosen* to make it difficult. Meditation has shown me this. One of the most practical reasons I can offer for meditating is that it will make your life much easier.

When we face a problem in our lives with our conscious mind alone, we bring all our fears, worries, guilts, attachments, and short-range desires to bear in the decision-making process. When we apply the tool of meditation, however, we tap that altruistic aspect of ourselves that is committed to joining with others for the betterment of the whole world. We also connect to the long-range picture and gain a wider perspective on our problem and its importance in our life. We gain access to not only what will serve us best at this time, but what will serve us best in the long run. Additionally, we have the bonus of knowing that our decision may benefit all humanity. As we find peace within ourselves, we help our brothers and sisters around the earth to find peace as well.

In my practice of meditation it has helped me to think in terms of my "conscious mind" (which serves a certain part of reality) as being the size of a keyhole, and my less-conscious awareness as being the size of a whole mansion. The keyhole that represents my conscious mind is also covered with layers of screens—the products of my past conditioning. The mansion which represents my less-conscious awareness contains the larger picture that is possible, unobstructed by previous conditioning. By meditating we can step into our mansion and enjoy the opportunity to experience the larger part of ourselves that is joined with everything, the part of us that has existed since the dawn of time, the part of us that continues without end.

> *My discovery of the meditation game:*
> When I first decided I wanted to meditate,
> I judged that I wasn't doing IT . . .
> That I must *go someplace out there*
> *to get it from someone*
> *who had it!*

Meditation was just one more thing to add to my list of things I needed to be happy. I set about to acquire it just as I would go after any other desire. I didn't feel I could afford the $600 "special" by the local guru, so I started asking: "How did *you* learn to meditate?" For answers, I got mystic rituals, secret methods, diets, arcane systems, sacred techniques, dos and don'ts, can'ts, musts, and impossibles!

I felt overwhelmed in this most occult territory; the

mysterious rites of initiation seemed so difficult to explain so that I could understand. I decided that meditation must be for a privileged few, and this decision only reinforced my belief in my less-than-holy status. I resigned myself to await the blessing from on high that would announce my readiness to partake in this most sanctified state. In other words, I gave up on being one of the "chosen ones" for the moment. But while I was cultivating my conscious self-doubt, I unconsciously planted the seed that started the whole process unfolding: I *asked* to be able to meditate.

Even though I was sure that nothing was happening, the process had started which would provide me with what I wanted. A chance enrollment in a yoga class was the answer to my felt request, though it took me awhile to recognize this subtle, oblique process at work. Although my conscious mind was convinced of my lack of ability to meditate, other levels of my awareness were guiding me into a practice that would eventually free me to discover many beautiful things about myself.

My conscious mind was very clever—it thought it had all the exits and entrances to my deeper awareness guarded and blocked. My censor worked overtime to keep *only* familiar, mundane information flowing in and out. All other information was properly and promptly labeled, filed, and sealed lest it confuse the "master plan" at work. And the "master plan" was killing me, bit by bit, the slow, painful torture that only the true "victim" personality has the opportunity to know well.

My "poor me" had managed to be so sick and in such pain that I couldn't be expected to do what other people did. Subconsciously, I sought reinforcement for my self-diagnosis as a useless victim who needed a lot of help from others to survive. Here are some examples of how labeling myself as a victim resisted new input that would alter the "master plan."

I was free of most physical and mental pain with my wish for health at age seven, but by age nine migraine headaches came crashing in. I can still remember the fear of going blind as my visual field narrowed. I walked home in the glare of bright sun reflected off snow with a searing pain throbbing in my head that increased as I stopped every few feet to vomit. The repressed emotions of an achievement-oriented "good little girl" were screaming to be heard. The migraines continued, getting worse as time went by. When I started the yoga class I was resigned to back spasms that kept me from lifting my first two sons throughout their toddlerhood. My midback was so tight at times that I had difficulty breathing and couldn't distinguish spine and ribs from muscle fiber.

My conscious mind continued to follow the track it had chosen, full of the fear of what lay in store for me and even more fear of changing. I was in my late twenties, had arrived at the top of my profession, I had borne two wonderful sons—and I was miserable. What was wrong with me?!

As I look back, that one little request to meditate was the point of a major shift in my life. Because my mind was keeping a tight guard on my narrow view of life, my body helped me out. And, as my body started to flex, so did my mind. As my body eased its pain, so did my mind. A process began which continues to this day, at this writing, sixteen years later. The only difference is that my mind, spirit, body, and emotions now cooperate and acknowledge their oneness, and they have let their guards down a little. Yoga means "yoke" or "union" and was indeed the unifying practice that I received when I asked for meditation. I got what I truly wanted and needed on all levels of my consciousness.

Be absolutely clear on this point. I am *not* saying that yoga is *the* only way to enlightenment; it was the answer to *my* sincere request for a positive change. It was my first conscious embarkation point into a consistent, fearless relationship with my other levels of awareness. Your point of departure from fear can be anything that suits your unique being. All you need to find it is the intention and commitment to let go of your less-desirable ways of dealing with life.

As I started my yoga practice, I set aside an hour to

myself each morning before the children got up and later added a quiet hour after work, in the bathtub, with no interruptions. I called these sessions "morning yoga" and "relaxing and cooling down from a stressful job." Accompanying these dramatic changes in my schedule were a parade of rich and memorable dreams, as well as a wonderful spacey feeling I tuned into every time I immersed my hands in warm dishwater and gazed through the window to the fields beyond. This spacey feeling began to happen at other times, as well, and I eventually realized it was actually a form of meditation.

A few years later the dreams turned out to be prophetic. I also learned how to consistently summon the spacey feeling at will, and this "alone time" became a habitual practice before making decisions or acting on them. It slowly dawned on me that maybe I was doing something like "meditation" in my life.

Yet, at the same time I was still busy criticizing myself by comparing myself with others. I didn't *feel* like others who were meditating *looked;* I still seemed to be aware of my surroundings, I wasn't getting all the answers my friends did, and I didn't even have a consistent practice established, complete with candles and incense, as so many others I knew did.

When I first tried to meditate I used mandalas, mantras, whatever anyone suggested. I'd lie on my back (the back pain was still too great to sit up), immediately fall asleep, and wake up feeling frustrated. Someone suggested that I clean my channels; so, okay, at least it was something concrete. Every day I would visualize an aperture to a *tunnel*, like a doorway or an entrance to a cave, and I'd clean it with toothbrushes, cleanser, soap, mops, scrub brushes, even dynamite . . . depending on my mood and patience at the moment. I'd cry and beg to be let into the inner circle of meditators. I couldn't quite achieve the *ideal I had set up in my head* . . . and there it is—the *real* stopper—*my expectations*. It had to *be* a certain *way* or it *wasn't right!*

To add to my difficulties, I had, at the time, a close

friend who meditated beautifully. Every time I had a question, she would meditate and immediately give me an answer. This only served to increase my *belief* that I couldn't do it for myself. There was a positive side to this, too, as my belief in the meditative process and my trust in the power of the meditative state increased spectacularly. Each time I asked my friend specific questions and received direct, useful answers about life patterns, goals, spiritual truths, and even how to relieve poison oak, my skeptic eased a little and I was able to let go of some blocks in my long-clogged channels. I saw problem after problem arise and be handled with ease and growth and with a sense of rightness for all concerned.

I also saw meditation used to manipulate inexperienced spiritual seekers. Many of these followers were willing to follow power-hungry new age hype-types who were transferring their need for power in the workaday world into the spiritual realm. A friend calls such people "Mookta Hooktas." These "experts" set themselves up by implying that they have a pipeline to the *real* answers; thus, we should surrender without question to their mastery rather than find answers through our own efforts. There is plenty of precedent for such exploitation: thousands of years of master/follower and church/state power games can be an intimidating heritage to challenge.

It is time to let go of the intermediaries between "God" and you. It is time to take full responsibility for listening to our inner guidance by practicing meditation. Meditating for ourselves, discovering our own answers, finding our commonality with all peoples—this is the "spiritual revolution," the "second coming," the "Aquarian Age," the "end of the world," and so on. This is IT and IT is here and now and has been for some time. The big revolution is deceptively quiet and informal, as are most simple and beautiful truths. It is within us all and accessible through meditation.

We can save ourselves years of denial by hearing the simple truth above. I didn't recognize it when I was actually meditating because I was trying so hard to do it like someone else. Now, when people ask me how to meditate, I first ask them to find a place in their lives where they are already experiencing meditation without recognizing it (mine was the spacey feeling I got while doing dishes). Perhaps you are meditating when you are walking or running, gardening, driving, when you think over your day, as you enjoy a cup of coffee, whenever you sit in a certain chair, or when you philosophize about the world.

Tension is life; the absence of tension is death. When we quiet our body/mind by meditating, we provide a natural balance for the tensions that build up in our life. Tension followed by relaxation is a healthy, natural cycle, but in our busy, modern society we are more familiar with tension as a constant part of life. Tension followed by more tension is definitely *not* healthy, anymore than is the sustained contraction of a muscle. Thus, meditation is conducive to health as it maintains an appropriate cycle of tension and relaxation.

Meditation is already in action in our lives no matter how subtly it may manifest. To find it, we can examine the areas of our lives that are going as planned and/or expected. Usually, success is taken for granted, or looked on as luck, because that part of life seems so smooth. With a bit of introspection, we can determine where the seed of success was planted and find that here is fertile ground for planting the seed of contemplation, perspective, and awareness, needing only recognition and nurturing to come to full bloom. Here we also find an approach to life that is already successful. From here it is a simple step to apply the process in other areas of life. I found my place when I realized that I had been bringing peace and perspective into my life for years while doing dishes. With that conscious discovery and the model for meditation it provided it was very easy to transfer that feeling and experience to other times of the day.

Meditation is a simple act. The more ceremony we surround it with, the less likely it is that we will integrate it into our lives. It is a highly desirable tool for problem-solving, clear thinking, relaxing, communicating, and maintaining peace of mind amidst the turmoil of our modern world. I ask you to ignore the popular idea that it is a mystical rite inaccessible to most, initiated by privilege, or bought into like a lottery, as I once believed. There is really only one ingredient . . . TIME! Even if you don't think that you can find the time to meditate in your current schedule, begin somewhere. Take thirty minutes, fifteen minutes, even two minutes, but begin. As you begin to meditate and experience some of the benefits you will *make* more time for it.

One thing that stopped me from enjoying my meditation experiences was my expectation of what I *should* be *seeing*. There are as many ways to perceive images through meditation as there are people. And some people tell me they don't *see* anything . . . they *feel*, or *hear*, or *smell*. Take what is there for you and let it come forth as it wants. Have no expectations. Take as long as you want. It is a rare individual who sees an image like a moving picture on the silver screen. My most profound visions have come in ten-to-twenty-second flashes that may take thirty minutes to describe adequately in words, and many hours to write out.

Meditation, like any other skill, takes practice, and it may take hours, weeks, or even years to reach new depths of understanding. It is a lesson in dropping habits, and learning to let our minds run free, without constraints. Until we realize that we can direct this marvelous energy we will be a victim of the limitations of our mind.

For the past sixteen years I have used two water images to help me let go of past regrets and future expectations and be fully in the present moment. They are a preparation for and lead-in to meditation, and can take us to a place where we can open to our deeper wisdom with less mind chatter. These images can be very helpful for your ongoing practice. Make a commitment to use them and set a schedule to fulfill it. It takes only a few minutes a day. Start *now!* You may find it useful to read them into a tape recorder and play them back as you relax.

THE BRIDGE OF RELEASE

Sit or lie on your back.

Close your eyes or look down into your lap with your eyes loosely focused.

You are standing on a Bridge.

Water is streaming below. Feel it. Smell it. Hear it.

For now, throw into the water: troubles, cares, worries, guilt, resentment, fear, anger, people, anything that comes to mind at this moment. The idea is to let go only for a moment, not necessarily permanently.

Let these troubles float downstream, away from you, around a bend. Then see yourself standing on the Bridge with light pouring from you. Beams of light flow out in all directions as far as you can imagine . . . out to loved ones, around our world, out into the universe. Visualize others with light flowing out of them also; see your lights joining. The more light is sent out, the more is generated . . . An unending supply from within us all.

A LEAF IN THE WATER

Sit or lie on your back.

Close your eyes or look down in your lap with your eyes loosely focused.

A stream of water is pouring off the ice melt from a mountain top. The water flows through the ice and on down the side of the mountain. As the water moves through the timberline, following the bends and turns of the land, a leaf falls into the stream. It bobs and moves with the flow of the water.

Follow the leaf. Notice every detail.

Now . . . *you* are the leaf. Let yourself be moved by the water. The leaf floats on all the forms of flowing water that you can think of: ponds, rushing rapids, water-falls, lakes, large rivers, whirlpools; ultimately, even the ocean.

The leaf never gets stuck for long. Each time it is snagged, the force of the water moves it on its way—the leaf is always bobbing along the top.

The Bridge and the Leaf and be used anytime, day or night. Whenever I become aware that I am getting contracted with worry or guilt, or feeling invaded by others' energy, I call up one of these images and smile as I feel the release they bring to my whole body.

I have come up with a variation of the "Bridge" that is particularly useful when you are feeling burdened by anxieties. I tended to carry around my troubles and responsibilities like a suitcase full of rocks. One day it struck me how silly it would be to see someone carrying around a suitcase full of clothing, food, toilet paper, baby pictures, the vase mother sent, or whatever they feared they might need at any moment. I was being just as silly, carrying around my worries about my children, taxes, finances, relationships, and health, even though I couldn't do anything about any one of them at the moment.

I started examining these concerns more closely to understand why I carried them around so much. With my children in particular I had fears about their safety when they weren't with me. I'd worry about fires, earthquakes, falls, and incompetent doctors and I succeeded in scaring myself. So I began putting them into a boat with a life-guard and sending them downstream. They had a wonderful time and I felt pounds lighter. I went through my tote bag of troubles one by one and in this way began the process of letting them go. Throwing off the bridge doesn't have to be a violent act; in fact, it can be one of the most loving acts we ever perform in our relationships. Holding on causes strain for all concerned.

I could feel the difference in both my body and mind immediately. Though I had been carrying these burdens around mentally, my body also reacted by straining as if carrying a heavy physical load. After this, I began suggesting in classes that people put their loved ones in satin-padded boats with a loving nanny and ease them all into the water for a peaceful, happy ride.

When I was a teacher in the classroom I threw my students and co-workers off the bridge regularly. I will never forget a lovely young woman who did the bridge visualization. She sat up quickly, exclaiming, "Oh, no! I just threw my grandmother off the bridge!" She was horrified that she had done such a thing. We talked and I explained to her that this is what it is all about. Her grandmother was very ill and the family was taking turns at her bedside; they believed she would die soon. I suggested that when she was with grandma, be with her one hundred percent, and when away from her, trust the other family members to care for her and send her love. I further suggested that she might teach grandma to throw things off the bridge, as she may have a few to toss herself.

I love these two images for letting go of mental burdens and for going with the flow of life and the universe. Sometimes I spend a great deal of time with the details of each image. Other times, just the thought of the image brings a smile and a lighter feeling. After many years of friendship with the bridge image, it now comes to mind instantaneously when I am in a tense situation. It allows me to gain perspective on my immediate situation, and to let go of my expectations about of how the situation *should* be played out. I use it to let go of belief systems, or things and people I identify with. It facilitates a continual cleansing and growing process for me.

Daily practice with these images has allowed me to discard old tapes of ways I thought things had to be done, and continued use has given me new responses to replace old ones. The new responses provide me with an awareness of the larger picture, and give me the pause I need to collect the larger part of me that sees long-range effects. In most cases it takes about ninety days to change even a simple habit, such as the way we brush our teeth, to the point that we know we will not slip back. So when I talk about generations of conditioning as a victim, for example, I am very respectful of the ingrained programming we must deal with.

Meditation can serve us in many ways; one door leads to another. It can be used in many capacities to suit our lifestyle. Meditation is a creative art and a practice that must be flexible in order to accommodate our changes as we grow. After starting with some practical, day-to-day applications I hope your curiosity will be stimulated enough to give it a try. I've been told that meditation is addictive. Maybe so. It would be nice to be addicted to something that feels so good and for which you have an unlimited supply that costs nothing. With practice you will learn that the resources are within us all and are freely available at any moment.

Meditation has helped me work with what I call my "divergent-path syndrome." I would clearly figure out in my conscious mind exactly what I wanted to be doing and then I would watch in exasperation as my own actions sabotaged my plan. There seemed to be an ongoing conflict between my conscious mind and a less-conscious part of my awareness that had equal power over the outcome of my plans. Having learned not to blame others, I was now left with the task of not blaming myself. I wanted to find a way to take full responsibility for all of my desires, motivations, and actions on all levels of awareness. I wanted to get to know this less-conscious part of myself intimately. To do this, I took the following steps:

1. I *watched* my actions, trusting that there is a reason somewhere in my being for doing what *seems* to be against my wishes at the moment.

2. I *respected* the needs of the less-conscious part of me as *valid*, and as fulfilling some deep need that I may not understand or even acknowledge with my conscious mind.

3. I *accepted* the actions I chose to take, and then looked deeply into the part of me that seems to *need* to go in another direction from what I think I want.

Once I acknowledge my full plan, I can find the intelligence operating behind the scenes. But if I keep denying that there is an alternative plan, there is nothing to work with, so I stay caught in blaming something or someone else. One clue to lack of movement is a feeling of being in a squirrel cage that is going round and round. I eventually tire of the endless circles and look for a way to spiral out.

An example that most of us can identify with is "trying" to diet. Thousands of pounds are gained and lost in diet programs. When I attempt to lose weight, I know that a part of me wants to lose weight, while a stronger part of me is invested in some way in keeping weight on this body. Until I get in touch with the reason(s) for holding onto excess weight and respond appropriately to those reasons, I have no hope of losing weight and keeping it off.

We are all part of a universe composed of cycles, harmony, rhythms, seasons, plans, and many facets, and *not* a one-directional arrow that simply needs pointing to accomplish something. We need to honor our whole universe and quit attempting to "fix up" some defective part. We are a complex matrix, an elaborate, tangled, beautifully designed, and sometimes confused web. If we treat ourselves more like part of an orchestra and less like a solo artist, we may come to a happier appreciation of our complexity.

Attempting to *control* our personal universe is not the answer. It is as fruitless and frustrating as if a cell in my hand were to say, "I don't want to go," when my hand reached up to scratch my face. Luckily a cell doesn't have such power. Can you imagine the chaos that would ensue if we had to have a consensus vote of all the cells in a hand every time we wanted to move it?

On some level of awareness it is this type of confusion in our body/mind communication that causes physical paralysis and lack of coordination, or in the mental paralysis of ambivalence. We can say "No! I'm not going to move" all we want, but when the earthquake comes we *will* be moved. The earth does not consult us when it wants to have a quake. (Or is it that we are too busy to hear the earth talk to us? The animals seem to know.)

We are individuals and we are a part of this magnificent order of the universe from the tiniest microbe to the ant hill to the infinite order of outer space. Human history is a dance of political and religious organizations attempting to have power over time, change, nature, and resources. They all cycle through the blush of birth, the excitement of growth, and the pain of decline and death. Each political and religious organization is going to be the system that beats the cycle, yet in time they all succumb to the rhythm of life and the recycling process that is a part of the larger picture.

We *can* become aware of our connection to all with our conscious minds. When we feel that our intentions don't match the needs of others, it is time to check in with our inner guidance by meditating and get a look at the whole picture. This will reveal the nature of others' plans and show us how we can blend with the united whole instead of fighting it. We *can achieve* our personal goals *and harmonize* with our surroundings. When all of our awareness is available, we can either sit quivering in fear and defensiveness, and plot to control our universe so we will feel safe, or we can *befriend* a universal plan by getting to know it better. Meditation is my way of getting better acquainted with as large a picture as I can and of blending with it without losing my individuality.

Secretly I know that

Only a small part of me
    has been taken by the needs
        of the frightened others
            who raised and taught me
                as they had been taught.

Only a small part of me
    has bought the need to compete
        and kill my brothers and sisters
            for an economic illusion.

Only a small part of me
    believes my drama
        is created by others
            outside my design.

There is another, larger part of me
    that knows unconditional love
        and is joined to all.

Meditation is the opening space
    allowing passage to a larger part of me
        which contains my sense of humor
        and my sense of well-being.

The *how* of meditating:
    Take time
    Be physically comfortable
    Breathe
    Let go of mind clutter
    Listen
    Enjoy

The *why* of meditating:
    To touch the sacred
    It's fun
    To gain perspective
    To break patterns

The *when* of meditating:
    Anytime
    When I lose my sense of humor
    When I feel my anger rising

The *where* of meditating:
    Anywhere

The *what* is up to you.

7 Other Channels to Fuller Awareness

I use several methods to deepen my meditation. They vary according to how I feel at the moment, the purpose of the meditation, and how much time I have allowed for it. I have experimented to find the methods that work best for me; these methods are tailored to my uniqueness and personal needs. I have found that difficulties encountered in meditation, both by me and by others, generally fall into three categories:

1. Using someone else's technique, which fits as poorly as someone else's clothing.
2. An overly idealized expectation of what the meditative state is and what it can do for the meditator.
3. Failing to make meditation a high enough priority.

In fact, the entire process of effective meditation can be as simple as prioritizing the brushing of our teeth. Most of us do this daily, maybe even several times a day. We somehow find the time for it in our busy schedules. Why do we schedule and prioritize this activity so well? Because it is *important!* How do we know that it is so important? Because parents, teachers, dentists, billboards, health councils, and helpful others have told us it is important from the time we had teeth to brush.

Yet how much encouragement to meditate have we received from any of these authorities and role models in our lives so far? Has a feeling of urgency to meditate been conveyed to us by anyone? Have any dire consequences been predicted for failure to meditate? Did anyone offer to do it with us to be sure we'd learn to do it right?

If I suggested you needn't brush your teeth you may say, "But I would get holes in my teeth if I didn't brush them!" That may be so, but consider the painful holes in our emotions, mental processes, spirit, and soul. Are there more people suffering from pain in their teeth or pain in their relationships to life? When we have pain in our teeth, most of us go immediately and without question to a dentist. Where do we go to soothe the aches and pains of loneliness, confusion, and fear?

If I had to choose, I'd meditate with the three minutes that I now spend brushing my teeth. (You'll be happy to hear that I find time for both.) Don't miss the point: it is the *priority* we give to meditation and the *intention* to do it, not method or technique, that will result in creating a regular meditation practice.

I think one of the reasons we avoid meditation is that we liken it to inactivity or laziness—someone sitting around "contemplating their navel." But meditation *is* an active state. Besides, we don't have to *achieve* and *do* all of the time.

I also hear people say they can't meditate, when, in fact, what they really mean is that they don't want to meditate. But this is all right—there is sanity in saying to ourselves, "I don't want to do that," just because it doesn't feel right, even if it defies logic. It isn't necessary to blame someone or something for not doing something we don't want to do. We convince ourselves of our own stories and then we are in trouble. It is much more harmonious for my personal universe for me to say, "I don't want to right now," rather than, "I can't because . . . " The "I can't" translates into, "I'm a failure with no power over my life, a victim of circumstances beyond my control." This is what our insides are hearing us reinforce every time we make an excuse. Just listening to what we are saying to ourselves is such a marvelous way to get to know ourselves.

If you want to meditate, then meditate. Forget your excuses of not knowing how. Excuses for not meditating are just as empty as a complaint of not knowing how to diaper a baby. I suggest the same solution to both problems—practice. Just do it the best you can and it will be the right way for you. To diaper a baby you need one baby plus one diaper plus practice and this equals success. For meditation you need to set aside the time plus listen plus practice and this equals success. In fact, the meditation formula may be the easier of the two.

When I have decisions to make, I meditate to contact my inner guidance. At times I have changed my mind at the last moment on the strength of this guidance, without even knowing "why." Sometimes there is confirmation ahead, such as a wreck on the road I was about to take; usually, however, there is no obvious confirmation. The value of this guidance is simply the trust and confidence I gain each time I respect the decision-making process of my whole being, rather than relying solely on my logic and will.

Meditation is no longer an isolated process, but an integral part of my daily life. The following methods are practices I have evolved in meditation to increase my understanding and appreciation of the magnificence of our less-conscious awareness and our connection with the whole universe.

IMAGING AND VISUALIZING

When faraway friends are ill or in need in some way we often feel helpless. The following exercise is a means of reaching them on a more spiritual level. It can also increase our confidence in being able to communicate with others at a distance. I also find that it helps me to expand, rather than contract my feelings, as well as to gain a broader perspective.

> Visualize yourself standing on a hill. A light source within you starts to shine, radiating out as far as you can think (use color with the light if you want). Light comes out of your fingers, toes, back, and chest and gets brighter and goes further with each breath. The more you send, the more seems to be generated. There is no end to the supply.

Sometimes I think of specific family members and friends and enfold them with this light. Other times I move geographically, starting with my home and extending to city, state, country, continent, across oceans to other areas of the world, the whole earth, the solar system, deep space, and beyond.

Giving is receiving and receiving is giving. As we send love and light we also receive love and light. By the very act of offering, we will also receive. As we shine our light out, we cleanse ourselves and release whatever has blocked this light. This gives us an open and expanded feeling, somewhat like the expression, "I feel larger than life," in the sense of feeling generous, full of life, and on top of our problems. We feel in charge when we have something to give, and we can always give love and light from our never-ending supply.

I have heard older people express feelings of uselessness because they can't give what they want to their grandchildren. People who are on limited incomes and believe they have nothing to give could learn something from Rose. Rose has seven children of her own and married a man with nine; almost all of these children have produced grandchildren. Rose sends birthday cards to them all, and stays in touch with other friends, just for the price of the postage and paper. She does this by copying the designs from other cards with crayons and writing her own loving

remembrance. I always feel honored and touched when I receive a card from her. This is not an idle lady of leisure—she runs a ranch full-time with her husband. I admire and appreciate her for ignoring the easy excuse she could be using not to connect with everyone.

Using Images to Enhance Meditation

Images are powerful tools. A few years ago, a small shift in the way I perceived myself provided some insight into how I valued my strengths. I had been delighting in my flexibility and the ease with which I seemed to float from one scene to another, adapting myself to the needs of others as I went. I saw others as rigid where I was bending until it occurred to me to consider the possible disadvantages of seeing myself as a feather tossed in the wind rather than as a rock amid the waves. By visualizing myself as a huge, solid rock anchored deep in the earth, I regained my lost power and stability. It became a delight to feel the waves of life crashing against me as my strength held firm.

The following image is a peaceful scene to visualize when your patience is being tested by being late or having to wait in long lines. I also follow this tranquil path into a deeper exploration of my other levels of awareness. It is a conscious way to enter the areas we usually only visit in the dream state.

I walk along a path I remember from the past or a new one I am creating right now. The path can be in a city, in the country, or even in outer space if I want. I walk along the path, feeling it with my feet, smelling the air, becoming aware of the entire environment through all of my senses. I notice everything alongside the path and beyond. Often I add water in some form. I keep walking and sensing in this way until I come to a comfortable place where I sit down. I bathe in the peaceful scene I have created for myself, or allow my fantasy to continue. I may create more adventures along the path or simply enjoy the peace of this quiet space.

Once on this path, I found myself on a trail that led along ridges from one snowy mountain top to another. It was a well-worn trail in the ice and I was following an extremely long line of fellow travelers. We were all dressed alike and I couldn't tell which one was me. This image was most significant for me at the time because I had been asking for more freedom from my ego's interference.

I felt the answer to this request was, "I am on my path and it is an old one, trod by many before me, one that many will follow. There is no need to worry about the ego interfering. All is in order." Had I not undertaken this visualization or a similar one, I might not have heard this message so clearly, or experienced the peace it brought so profoundly.

You may wonder if I am making this up, either consciously or unconsciously. It doesn't matter. It is still the mind at work, and such information is there for each of us if we allow ourselves to explore. I offer a guided meditation at every class I teach and the variety of mental pictures students see is astounding. I love to ask people where they have gone after working with a suggested image; it is such an adventure to step into another's consciousness. It amazes me to see how much I presume others are experiencing a shared event as I have experienced it. By listening to others I am reminded that my view is only my perception and that I should never presume to know another's interpretation.

AWAKENING AT NIGHT

Periodically, I awaken at a consistent time in the middle of the night. I used to fret about the loss of sleep, spending my awake time worrying about its consequences. Then I decided to accept this wakefulness as a gift of time I had given to myself. After all, I often complained during the day that I never had enough uninterrupted time.

Now I take advantage of this gift of time with great appreciation. I read, write letters, work on my journal, or prepare for the coming day, and I do it all with joy and lightness. Sometimes I feel tired the next day but what I accomplished during the night usually lightens my work load. And the tiredness is worthwhile in light of the knowledge that I asked for this special time, so I usually sleep well the next night. With a little conscious programming I can even feel refreshed the next day, rather than succumbing to being tired because I lost a little sleep. I simply suggest to myself before I drift off to sleep that I awaken fully rested and ready for my day. Yes, it works, and if I feel a need I can get a whole nap full of rest in a few minutes of deep relaxation.

Aside from getting caught up with, or even ahead of, my work, I have found other needs are met by this gift of time. It is a marvelous time for meditating. The atmosphere seems clearer, perhaps because most people are sleeping and their mental turmoil is quieted for awhile. I am alone with my energy; able to sense how I can be more sensitive to it and even play with it. In fact, most of this book has been written between 3 and 6 AM and it has been a process full of great contentment, joy, alertness, uninterrupted clarity, and concentration.

SURRENDERING

Letting go of the way I think things have to be has become a meditative practice for me. As I let go of my expectations, I obtain a greater perspective. From this greater perspective, it is as if I transport myself to the top of a mountain where I can see how to put all the pieces in order. Thus, the "mistake" I was sure would happen if I did the "wrong" thing can now become part of the perfect order of things.

READING

I often read something inspirational such as magnificent poetry, a philosophical thought, or an uplifting autobiography. This stimulation helps me envision higher goals for my personal potential, and unlimited possibilities seem more attainable. I am able to open to more expansive thoughts of what I am and what I can do, and my intention to achieve my goals is clarified and strengthened.

Reading can guide me into a meditative state. This is another example of a time that I had been meditating for years before I identified it as meditation. I would read a little and then float somewhere between the lines, out into other dimensions. Sometimes these wanderings are related to what I'm reading and sometimes any correlation is vague at best. You may even find yourself drifting into the same meditative process as you read this book.

MAKING MUSIC

Music is highly recognized as a universal language. It is something I have been passionately drawn to all my life. And through music I was often experiencing what I discovered later to be a meditative space that felt wonderfully comfortable. Making music with others is a rich way to join with others in an atmosphere that is much like a group meditation.

When I wrote "Sing With Joy," I listened carefully to the words I was using and realized that I was programming my life with them. I had cleaned up my speaking vocabulary quite a bit by letting go of "can't," "should," "need," "try," and many others that tightly defined my boundaries. I then realized that I was favoring songs with sad lyrics written in minor keys—songs full of victim stories about "maids of constant sorrow" whose lovers left them with the dishes to wash and the kids to care for. It had become a habit to sing songs that were sad, oozing negative emotion. I said a firm "no" to lyrics about a poor victimized me, changed my words *and* tunes, and let my passions flow through joy, love, and life. I started a new habit of singing about love and joining and lightness and, sure enough, I began feeling the passion of sharing and the joy of uplifting peace and humor.

SING WITH JOY

Sing with Joy, Joy, Joy._____
Sing with Love, Love, Love.____   Sing for peace with-in _____ your-
Sing with Life, Life, Life. ____

self._ The journey can seem so long,_ but on the way we can sing a

song._ So let's hear our voi-ces to-day_ I know you have plen-ty to

say_ Hey_ sing a-long with me now__ I love to show you

how_ The words flow from the heart Come on and take a part._

2. So we move along our road
   Shaking loose that heavy load.
   Let's cross the bridge, go over the next ridge,
   Turn a page, have a rage, become a sage.
   Unconditional love is so fine
   Flows out of your heart right into mine.
   So turn to someone brand new
   And tell them, "Hey, I love you too."

3. So if holding on is causing you pain
   Come on in out of the rain.
   Use the garbage can for anger and fear
   And your heart will feel more clear.
   Take a balloon trip to outer space
   See the love shining on your face.
   Open to peace of mind
   And healing you will find.

Music has been teacher, friend, and meditation partner for me. I continue to open to the muse for further revelations as I am ready to receive them.

LISTENING TO OTHERS

A wonderful way to get in touch with your inner guidance is to visualize a scene and bring in a person to help you. I call these people that come to help me my inner teachers. They appear in different guises at different times, taking the form of a friend, one of my children, an admired figure from history, someone from the future, or a being from another planet. Sometimes the form taken is not human at all; my inner teacher may be a rock, plant, fish, cloud, sunset, or just a feeling.

I formulate a clear question or problem, being as specific as I can in the moment. I close my eyes and visualize a path I have traveled to a bench where I now sit. A figure comes toward me and sits on the bench with me. I share my concerns with this person and we discuss them together. Often this person gives me an answer I have been seeking.

The process of asking and listening for answers serves to stop my habitual patterns of solving problems. It helps me tune into my less-conscious awareness where I can usually gain a larger perspective on my latest "problem." Frequently, I will find here another choice I haven't considered, or reinforcement for the rightness of my chosen path.

Another, less changeable, group of entities has been with me most of my life: I call them my spiritual helpers. They act like a committee with a tough project to complete; they have taken on roles that gently nudged or even firmly suggested courses of action for me at times when I believed I was powerless and a victim of circumstances. They have been the bigger and stronger part of me that leads when I feel weak.

These guides are available to us all. They are systems: we can let them go when they have fulfilled their service to us. They are able to share with us from a larger, more impersonal sphere of being. Because they are not caught up in mundane concerns, they can help us to see the broader perspective of any situation. This larger perspective is free of judgments; it does not contain right or wrong, or good or evil, as we have learned it with our conscious minds. No fear lies in this vast playground. No cloud of defense obscures our clear vision. Our spiritual helpers can take us to the very best of ourselves. Mine have acted as translators for a part of my awareness I was afraid either did not exist or was lost to me.

Two helpers have been especially significant at times of drastic change and growth in my life. Michael has been with me since I discovered the "M" in the lines of my palms. Michael doesn't talk, is very gentle, and his messages come straght to my heart. Michael is like St. Michael—a guardian angel. I don't think I have ever received a message from him that didn't cause me to weep with recognition and appreciation.

Emily, my other helper, tried to get my attention in 1973 and I ignored her. Her energy seemed so strong and blunt that I wasn't sure that I wanted to hear what she might reveal to me. Finally, in the fall of 1977, I allowed her presence to influence me. At that time I felt her hands at my back, telling me to start moving with my work *right now!* The hands were gentle and insistent, and they pushed with a sureness and strength that left no doubt that a message was coming from another part of my awareness. My work badly needed definition but I felt hesitant and self-conscious about what to call it. The only thing that seemed clear was that I was to help others recognize their deeper levels of awareness so that they could learn to make peace of mind a reality and a constant in their lives.

Emily was most patient with me. I kept waiting for someone to dub me "ready," to give me a certificate to practice. Emily gave me several clear messages that helped my focus. One was to write books that would share such ideas with others. She also suggested that I give a free class, open to all comers. At the time, this was a tough one to honor because I was very worried about how I was going to support my family. I did as she suggested, and as a result, learned a great deal about money as energy.

While giving the free class, my house was full of loving, supportive new friends hungry for spiritual nourishment. They didn't directly give me money, but somehow my money flow was no longer a problem and I found I had embarked on a career switch which still defies the logic of practical economics. Each month I was able to pay all my bills and still have some money left over.

My guides are still here with me, along with a host of others who boost me when I falter. They are my fan club. They cheer me on, laugh when I am silly, and serve as the hands that guide me back into the path when I stray. Though they aren't as strong a presence in my life right now, they are dramatic when they need to get my attention. Having gotten it, they remain more subtly present in my consciousness. I know they are there to be called upon when I feel a need for their guidance. (I will discuss my helpers further in the section titled "Envisioning," see page 133.)

STIMULATING THE CREATIVE FLOW

Our creativity can become stuck within the limits we place on ourselves, especially on our imaginations. I use the following image to break free of the limitations I may be experiencing in my physical world.

I find a beautiful meadow in my imagination; it can be one that I know or one I create. There I build a structure. I have at hand limitless supplies of materials, any helpers I want, and I don't have to adhere to natural laws like gravity. I have complete freedom and I allow my creativity to roam unfettered. I remind myself that my limitless imagination has full rein here.

This image allows complete mental freedom. Given all this liberty, it is fascinating to see where I allow my mind to wander and to notice the restrictions I impose on myself. What I do with this image reveals to me that I am setting limits; in this fantasy there is no one else to blame.

Once, when I did this practice, I started erecting a tower of prisms that caught the sunlight and dazzled the countryside. I kept adding on vertically and the tower grew higher and higher, like a huge stack of blocks. I felt myself becoming concerned about it toppling over, but then laughed when I remembered that I didn't have to follow gravity's dictates. My tower then became an undulating row of varied, sparkling shapes wending their way toward the sea.

The limitlessness of this image opens me to other means of creative expression such as singing, writing, painting, dancing, and more creative relations with others. When I feel limitless and creative, the patterns and ruts I usually fall into suddenly seem narrow and restricted. After experiencing creative limitlessness, I am moved to broaden my daily life patterns to include more creative space.

CONSULTING THE STARS

While this book urges you to give up labeling, I will now confess that I use astrology to help me deepen my meditations. Astrology appears to many as an example of blatant labeling, a system of categorizing people into personality structures according to the time of their birth, but it is much more. Astrology offers another matrix with which to experience an order to the universe. Most importantly, it helps me to remember what a deliberate and necessary part we all play in a larger plan.

Early in life, I absorbed a belief system in which only two choices for the organization of life processes existed: heredity and environment—the causes of our physical, mental, and emotional makeup. I remember violent debates on this issue in a psychology department which I eventually left because I felt it wasn't conducive to creative thinking.

Astrology can help us to release blame, cause-and-effect

thinking, and the "sins of the fathers," as we have known and practiced them. It guides us toward self-direction and self-responsibility from the first breath of life. According to astrology, each of us is fully in charge of the course of our lives; we are following a plan for the time we will spend here on earth. When reading peoples' charts, I simply point out their strengths, weaknesses, and their destiny and focus in this life. Usually there is recognition, if not immediate acceptance. It is interesting that most people I talk to are, in some way, apologetic for being here. They seem to be hiding their talents (even from themselves), feeling unimportant in the larger picture of life, and they are often dependent on the feedback of others for maintaining their self-image and self-esteem.

Astrology continually reminds me of our unique specialness as human beings. I often compliment people who have a particularly difficult chart for having taken on so much growth in this lifetime. They are brave and I support them in their learning process, even though it may seem like they are doing it the hard way; it is the way they have chosen to learn what they have planned to learn. In fact, we are all leading our lives according to the "right way" for ourselves.

Psychology is just now recognizing what most parents have known for centuries. Babies are born unique, with special personalities all their own. These budding personality structures continue on their unique path no matter what the parents do. For decades we have tried to place blame or give credit to a *cause* for the development of certain personality traits, only to find many inherent contradictions. For example, divorce is not necessarily *the* worst influence on a child; the child's conformity to its parents' expectations of what an acceptable child should be seems to be the only significant factor.

Beware of expectations. They can turn even a glorious sunset into a bothersome event if it doesn't match our anticipations. Expectations are a future constructed with the limitations from our past. If a couple has a quiet, receptive child, and that is okay with them, then the relationship works out well. They will raise a happy, quiet, and receptive person who feels worthwhile. But if an active, aggressive child is desired, they will only communicate their disapproval and anxieties to their passive little soul, who, in turn, will feel only disapproval and unworthiness.

While doing family charts, I point out the nature of the children and the gifts they bring to the other family members. Usually the parents recognize what I say, but they are not always able to adjust to the relationship in an understanding way. If that inability to bend and adjust is reflected in their chart, it is likely they will continue with the power struggle they are enmeshed in at the moment. At such times, I may suggest that while this is not bad it does indicate a relationship that is going about it the hard way. This is the means they have chosen to relate to one another, to learn and strengthen parts of themselves together in this family partnership.

Astrology often guides me to the reason behind the actions, where a choice can be made as to whether the action should be changed. Often, this understanding is all that is needed to attain some peace of mind. Astrology charts reveal life patterns that ebb and flow in cycles. They are not edicts etched in stone that are never to be challenged or changed.

JOURNEYING INTO OTHER TIMELESS REGIONS

A Past Life Regression takes us into our less-conscious awareness. It is accomplished by deeply relaxing and letting go of the conscious mind's control for a moment. The process brings up thoughts and emotions that are often deeply buried. It also allows the conscious mind to recognize the feelings that may be affecting us on other levels of consciousness.

In helping someone with a Past Life Regression, I ask the person to think of three areas they would like help with and then I tell them we will go to lifetimes that may shed some light on these concerns. Sometimes the images they experience are very clear and easily interpreted. Other times, not only are the images unclear, but neither of us can logically tie them to the person's immediate concerns. When this happens, we let it go; often, in time, the answer becomes clearer to the conscious mind. If we do nothing more than deeply relax and explore without fear and with trust in our other levels of awareness, we have spent our time well.

In my experience, anyone can explore in this way. The only people who seem to have difficulty are the "controllers" who can't let go even during this exercise. They will start to get an image and then abruptly return to full awareness. It's like watching someone who fears the depths attempting to swim underwater. They go down for a few seconds and then pop right back up like a cork. The urge to control is based on a fear of letting go or allowing anyone else to be in charge, even for a moment.

If it is not the right time for a regression, we let that be all right for now. I am mainly concerned that they trust in some part of their being that has a valid reason for not allowing them to probe these depths at this time. When the time is right they will be able to experience the process with ease and comfort. And perhaps knowing that part of their consciousness is on hold is the lesson they really needed.

Even those who say they don't believe in the concept of Past Life Regressions can have wonderful experiences if they want to. This process is very effective for bypassing our usual censors and reaching other levels of awareness.

Learning how to do Past Life Regressions for myself and others has given me a framework on which I could place a lot of feelings, thoughts, loose ends, unexplained phenomena, and confusion. I let them rest while I catch my breath and prepare for the next step in my growth.

BRINGING DREAMS TO CONSCIOUS AWARENESS

Another tool that comes to us from our less-conscious realms is the dream state. Messages from our dreams are easily used when we can remember the dream and interpret the action it represents correctly. Many good books are available that can help us learn to appreciate this state and learn to interpret its messages. Here are some suggestions to help you remember your dreams and gain insight through them:

1. Remember dreams by telling yourself before you fall asleep that you would like to become aware of what you are working on during sleep.

2. Read a dream book that discusses some of the universal symbols; it can help to broaden your interpretation and guide you in fathoming the meaning of your dreams.

3. Keep your interpretation open. Remember that the answer you receive is for this moment only. We learn our lessons in degrees, and the same dream can reveal many layers of a lesson over time. As in other forms of teaching, the teacher will remain and the lessons will continue as long as you don't close the door. Continue to respect the many levels of interpretation that are possible.

At times I want to remember and analyze my dreams in great detail, while at other times I feel satisfied with a general interpretation. There are even times when I don't want to hear anything from this realm. I feel that the conscious mind is the last to know what is happening in the depths of my less-conscious awareness. Most of the time I am content to let the less conscious part of me go about its business, unimpeded by my attempted translations.

My bodily functions do quite well without the conscious activation of each heartbeat, breath, or step; likewise, a whole inner level of awareness is efficiently processing my experience without my conscious intervention. Sometimes it is helpful to be aware of these spaces; other times it is better to simply trust—the information can and will be called to consciousness when the time is right.

When it's time to plumb my inner depths, my body shows signs of excessive tension and illness, I have accidents, or my mind manifests fear in one of its diverse forms: resentment, anger, guilt, worry, defensiveness, protectiveness, jealousy, or envy. At such times, when I ask the dream state to reveal some of the inner workings of my being that my conscious mind is refusing to recognize, it will reveal to me inner problems or needs that are not being met. I then gain a deeper understanding of those actions that seem to run counter to my conscious desires.

Some of my dreams have been prophetic and are usually a little confusing to interpret, though with hindsight, the interpretation can become clearer months or even years later. Why did I foresee certain events? Possibly part of my consciousness was preparing for the coming change—on some level I was adjusting and attuning already. It made me feel good to realize I was much more flexible than I had given myself credit for.

Trust in the profound wisdom of my less-conscious awareness has been growing. I have faith that a very large percentage of my being is already tuned into the changes coming up in my life. Only the conscious mind, with its investments in labels and belief systems, remains unattuned. The conscious mind is truly the last to become aware of the full process.

Before I move to a new house I usually have a strong impression of some part of the house or yard in my dreams that I easily recognize when I move; in my present home it was the woodwork. As soon as I saw it, the recollection and connection to my dreams of it were clear. Before a trip to Europe, I dreamt of a series of rooftops seen from the air. They were unusual: older, rounded, and peaked styles unfamiliar to me. The dreams made no sense until I stayed in a series of upper-floor bed-and-breakfast inns in

Europe. The view from these rooms looked out over the rooftops in my dreams.

Another time I dreamt of a series of quaint, Ivy-League-style campuses. This time I had it all figured out: I was going back east to do some work in local colleges. Wrong! I was invited to co-teach a class for teachers by a local university. Its architecture was modeled after that of a small, eastern Ivy League college. So you see, interpretations can be tricky. I suspect that even prophetic dreams are not meant to give us power over our future. They take place in the less conscious states of our being and I think they are doing their main work in those same areas. The conscious mind merely gets a glimpse now and then.

A recurring theme throughout my life, especially during the past fifteen years, has been a series of very graphic healing and cleansing dreams. They were so graphic that I hesitated to describe them here; however, I will offer some thoughts about them as I feel this is an area shared by many and discussed by few. The dreams were about overflowing toilets and not being able to find a clean, empty toilet. Their various meanings have ranged from being too full of old guilts and bad habits to feeling that my system was too full of junk, such as rich food, sweets, alcohol, environmental pollution, and smoke. These dreams have also pointed out that my house has been too full of furniture and other possessions, my mind too full of distractions, and my life too full of approving and disapproving people.

In many ways, these dreams were telling me to let go, release, flush it away, let it pass. From these cleansing dreams I learned that it wasn't what or how much I had in life but how much was getting in my way. My focus became clear when I saw that only *need* had to be disposed of, not people or things.

One of the most dramatic series of prophetic dreams I had concerned my last pregnancy. I was caught totally off guard by their message and learned a compelling lesson about categorization and labeling. The logical side of me had the following information to weigh and balance: I had two beautiful sons, ages eleven and thirteen, both delivered by Caesarean section. Two major surgeries seemed enough and I was worried because I had been on birth control pills for many years. My husband assured me that he wanted no more children. Armed with these facts, I decided to have a tubal ligation. Right after the operation, I felt a tremendous wave of sadness and depression, a deep, psychic ache within me. I can't adequately describe this feeling except to say I had a sense that something was very wrong. Almost immediately I began to dream about babies, little girls for the most part. They were all sizes and shapes; babies, babies, and more babies full of life and smiles. I looked forward to my dreams and the joy of spending each night with such delightful little lights.

Scrutinizing these dreams with the power of my logic, I was sure of the right interpretation this time: the babies were symbolic of my creativity. As it turned out, this was not entirely wrong; ten months later I conceived.

A psychic told my husband that he thought I had cancer because he saw cells multiplying very rapidly inside me. His logical mind was aware of the tubal ligation and this influenced his interpretation of what he was seeing. Only my dream state knew what was really happening. After I delivered a healthy son, the doctor said that the tubes looked like nothing had ever been done to them. They had completely healed. All of us were caught in the limitations of our logical thinking; only the open awareness of my dream state knew better.

ENVISIONING

Visions seem to come during dramatically passionate times in my life, to jolt me out of assumptions and illusions and guide me into vastly different ways of perceiving a given situation. I have always felt instant recognition of the truth at these times. Visions are very natural manifestations of our less-conscious awareness. They are similar to dreams except that they are played out when we are

fully awake. It's as if they can't wait until we sleep to share their wonderful revelations. The less-conscious areas of awareness are like a dinner in preparation in the kitchen. When the meal is ready it is served in the dining room. That is when the conscious mind gets to taste the results.

Because visions seem to come at times of crisis in my life, I have wondered if there was a way to experience the benefits more consistently. Over the years, my experience of these expansive feelings of truth, peace, and love has undergone a gradual shift in percentages. I started out feeling expansive, unconditional love about one percent of the time, and constricted, conditional, bargained love the rest of the time. The percentages have reversed now and are not always consistent. It ranges from feeling unconditional love and peace in my relationships around ninety percent of the time, to feeling pinching, stingy, controlling, fearful encounters about ten percent of the time. In addition, I can consciously shift the state of my being just by recognizing my participation in a constricted, conditional way of loving, but it can go both ways. I can be feeling wonderful, unconditional love but as soon as feelings of self-consciousness or pride in my achievement arise, I find myself wallowing in ego gratification and self-indulgence. It works the other way as well: when I am feeling contracted and competitive, the honest recognition of these feelings can bring about a reversal — then I smile at my armor and open to trust once again. Now the time I spend in the ten percent area is much shorter. Sometimes I just dip in, recognize where I am, realize I have a choice, and then I can transform the situation immediately. This way of being has emerged out of my willingness to recognize the visions I have probably had all my life for what they truly are.

Most of my visions usually seem like a time warp at the moment. They are quick flashes that last a few seconds in "reality," and leave their mark for the rest of my life. I'll share some visions that had an especially strong impact. They happened at a time when my former husband and I were contemplating separation. My mind was muddled with emotion. His role in the drama was "the guilt-ridden husband deserting his family for the true love of his life." My role in the drama was "the poor, pitiful, deserted wife and mother, the victim of another woman."

That was the plot in my conscious mind. On other levels, the reality was that we had finished this phase of our relationship, it was time to learn a new way of relating to one another. However, the nature of this separation, because of the other woman, was not acceptable to my conscious mind at the time. I had a lot invested in the relationship. I asked for help with this appalling drama: "Why is this happening? Please, isn't there another way?" The following vision was the response to this plea:

I was sitting in my living room watching TV late one night, awaiting my husband's return. I suddenly became aware of someone's presence in the room. A cold, shivery, fearful feeling swept over me. There was no sound. I didn't want to turn my head, but finally I did, just a few degrees to the left and I saw a man I recognized as Michael, my spiritual helper. I had never seen him before but I knew him immediately. He had brought his own rather large easy chair. He was sitting about eight feet from me with his head bowed down, arms limp, resting on the arm rests, much like Abraham Lincoln in his Memorial.

As I gazed at him my fear completely left me. I wanted him to speak or look at me but he just sat slumped in the chair, surrounded by a terrible aura of sadness. I felt a cold wave of fear flood through the inside of my spine once more. At this moment, the message became undeniable. It concerned the reality that I did not want to face, the change I was about to step into. The message was loud and clear, yet not a word had been exchanged: "This is not an affair to be patched up, this is truly the parting of our paths." And just that quickly and with that much understanding, at that moment, I accepted a devastating message with total comprehension and trust in its validity. I felt gratitude. It seemed so gentle and compassionate of the universe to have come to my level of understanding with the message and to have delivered it with such care for my tender feelings.

I went to sleep stunned but accepting.

Please take a delicate point here. My acceptance followed hearing a mysterious message that had been delivered; I accepted because my *total* being had heard and acknowledged it. Tremendous clarity awaits us when we can accept the perspective available from our less-conscious awareness. After this visit from Michael, I could feel both perfect peace and understanding of the whole situation, and, at the same time, on another level, I would still play the role of the deserted, resentful victim. It takes time for balance to make order out of the conscious mind's chaotic investment in how things are supposed to be.

The next day, as I related the experience to my husband, I vacillated between clarity and confusion as I worked to further integrate that larger perspective I had felt for one precious moment. I was determined that my conscious mind was going to come into alignment with my other levels of awareness.

The following vision happened during the same period, and provided a bit of help in restoring my sense of humor:

As I was sitting in my dining room, I saw, as if it were a play being acted out, an image of my husband and myself standing together and talking. Somehow, I could look at myself sitting and standing at the same time. I tingled all over as I began to realize what was transpiring. His lover came in and moved him around so that his back was to me. He was totally captivated by her, a loving gaze in his eyes. They embraced and my stomach grabbed tight as I sat watching the scene unfold. Facing me, she gave me the biggest and most deliberate smile and wink. I was a bit shocked and then we both smiled. Again no words transpired, but the message was perfectly clear: "I was your daughter in another life. I am here to help you let go of this person and move on with your life."

Here was another aid that helped me to let go by providing a dramatic vision that cut through all my conscious defenses.

Another vision I had was rather rude; in fact, *very* rude and sharp with me. It seems that the further along the path I travel, the less subtle the lessons become.

> I was lying on my back on the floor, feeling emotionally and physically exhausted and extremely sorry for myself. I was using one of my progressive relaxation techniques: my toes, the arches of my feet, the whole foot was bathed in the power of relaxation. Peace flowing through my entire body . . . feeling floaty, euphoric, peaceful, drifting away from the cares of life . . . When, THWACK!!! I saw a golf club being swung full force and striking the side of my head. The sound was especially loud and startling. I felt the impact on my temple through awareness, not through pain. I sat up. My adrenalin was flowing. My mind was racing. The message was again clear and unequivocal: "Get up and get going! You have much to do! Quit feeling sorry for yourself! Quit waiting for someone to make life happen for you! Get into action! Do it NOW!!!"

After my heart stopped pounding and my dignity was recovered, I laughed at the wonderful direct action of the message. I laughed even harder at the image of poor martyr me lying on the floor indulging in self pity.

One of my most peaceful and loving visions came when I desperately wanted some clarity on the purpose of my spiritual work. What was I here for? I wanted to be assured of my purpose and specialness in the world.

> I saw myself standing, gleaming and beaming, dressed all in white, with light radiating from me in all direc-

tions. As far as I could see stretched a khaki-colored landscape and the sky looked like a beige stage set. I saw people, in grave-size plots, in all directions, as far as I could see. The ground was a clay-like, sticky mud. Everyone and everything was the same khaki color, a color most disagreeable to me. People were sitting or lying in their plots which were outlined by loose ropes.

Once in a while someone would raise a hand in my direction, I would walk over to them, and they would stand. I would point out some steps, or another passage out of their area. They would move out of their plot by themselves, walk to me, and we would embrace. I noticed that none of the mud on their garments remained on mine. As they started walking away from me their inner light became brighter and brighter with each step they took. The khaki color vanished as these people became more gleaming and radiant. They walked until they were finally out of sight.

Again there were no words from on high, but the message was clear. The vision told me it didn't matter what I did. I would make certain connections with people during my life and we would help each other to stay radiant. I was to share with people only when they clearly and unmistakably asked. Their problems would stay with them until they chose to confront them, no matter what I did with or for them.

This was an important message at that particular time, because I felt impatient and wanted to heal the whole world, whether they wanted it or not. I was creating all kinds of confusion which diminished when I simply waited to be asked.

This vision continues to be meaningful to me. It is like a beautiful painting in which I see something new and more profound each time I look at it. At present, this vision is saying to me that we all have light within us that can be seen as soon as we look for it. The peace of joining is available to us at every moment.

My visions now come gently and subtly, as often as I

want. They come when I ask for clarification with a problem or help with something. My life is gentle now, no longer in turmoil, so I listen more carefully. The difference between my regular meditations and my visions are now subtle, as well.

Some of the interpretations from my visions may seem unrelated to you. Interpretations from visions and dreams are very subjective. The interpretation of a vision is often by a "feeling," though I can describe the result: it is a "knowing" that you have the "right" answer for you.

TRUSTING NOTHINGNESS

I allow myself a blank, open space that I have established through years of meditating. Here, the awareness of my bodily sensations decreases and my mind lets go of my daily routine. Here I feel a connection with all. Often I bathe in this space and have no conscious recollection or evaluation of the time or place I visited. I float in this space for a few minutes or an hour and come back when I feel a lift to a more conscious awareness of my surroundings. I feel refreshed and energized. When I have been disturbed by something specific, I go to this blank open space; then the confusion clears and I feel peace of mind return. Sometimes a very specific solution is presented after I come back from wherever my awareness has traveled.

Please keep in mind that the meditative practices I have described in this chapter are but a few of the techniques I use. Some are more applicable at certain times than others. Use them as guides in your own search. I know the channels that are right for me and I am open to new avenues. Let your feelings guide you to the ones that are right for you.

8 | Meditating and Joining with Others

Most of us are social beings who are always finding new reasons for gathering with others. Groups can be a powerful aid in reinforcing our new practices. I am suggesting that you can easily add another dimension to your existing group gathering or create a new group with the direct purpose of reinforcing your meditation practices. This section presents two ways to share in groups. The extent of detail given here is intended to help you to move to new dimensions of awareness through group participation and joining.

I have taught these group meditation and family meeting processes many times in workshops and retreats. Most people love using the techniques during the retreat but set them aside when they return home. Therefore, I'd like to emphasize that these suggestions, as with others in this book, will help maintain harmony and honest relationships in your life. They are like preventative medicine: if you use these techniques you may never know what illness you didn't get. The choice is yours—you can continue living from crisis to crisis, dashing about with rescue remedies to patch up each calamity, or you can choose a practice that will catch the crisis in the developmental stage and address it before it explodes in your face.

Before meeting with someone for an individual consultation or with a group for a retreat, I visualize, for a moment, the sign of infinity—a figure eight on its side. This reminds me that I am in the right place at the right time and so are all of the people with me. What we do together is a mutual decision, the choice of all involved, and it is in harmony with the rest of the universe. Gathering two or more together creates an opportunity for joining and a chance to participate rather than separate.

People have often commented about how loving and gentle my groups are. How do I find so many caring and sharing individuals and get them all to come together at one time? My answer is that in an atmosphere of trust and personal sharing the very best is drawn out of any of us. These are not *special* folks; they are people like you and me who have so much beauty hidden beneath layers of fear. When we gather with the purpose of *joining*, we open, expand, and reconnect with our innocence; thus, we can see it in others. And in this expanded state of purity, unmarred by knowing, we find a fresh outlook which has previously been hidden in the folds of our fears.

The crazies come to teach us too. We all have our own crazy sides and can find the seeds of another's craziness in ourselves, if we care to see them. The more angered and frightened we are by someone we have labeled "crazy," the stronger is the lesson they are here to teach us. Some of the most effective teachers at my retreats and workshops have been people who said exactly what was on their mind, even though it offended people at first. As the retreat unfolded, gratitude for this childlike honesty started to blossom among participants, which allowed us all to face the truth in ourselves.

Every group needs at least one person with a vision and the enthusiasm and energy to keep feeding it until it flares enough to light everyone's fire. A leader needs to know when to let go of the active leadership role and become simply the one who sustains the vision in a less active role. Using a group process for meditating will help the "leader" to listen and learn and will help the "followers" to assert and give. A group process helps us to recognize that we share leadership with each other along our various paths of growth.

At some point while facilitating groups, I ask the vocal ones to be quiet to allow space for the less vocal ones to check in verbally if they choose. The validity of doing this is continually reinforced by the pearls of insight that roll off the tongues of the quiet ones. Rich expressions, sometimes stifled anger, and passionate feelings would perhaps go unnoticed and unheard had I not allowed space for their expression. Legend says that some native Indian tribes had a five-minute interval after someone spoke during which no one was allowed to speak except the speaker. Imagine the peace, freedom, and security this process gives the speaker. Imagine the depths to which the speaker feels heard.

A BRIEF GROUP MEDITATION PROCEDURE

Here is a formula for a quick way to meditate with any willing group. It can be used in a classroom, with your family, at the office, with friends, for planning sessions, with multiple families and with any group that wants to experience joining. I find it especially good before a meeting where a little edginess is felt, when major decisions are being made, perhaps, or when two factions have opposing concerns that require a compromise. This meditation is particularly good in the morning or at the beginning of any gathering. It sets the tone for the entire day, sending everyone off with a helpful thought to replace the usual worries we carry around all day.

Suggestions for getting started:

1. Sit in a circle in chairs or on the floor.

2. Join hands and sing, say a verse, or sit in silence for twenty to thirty seconds.

3. Let go of hands and close eyes.

4. Each person thinks about what they would like help with for *this day*. Make the requests as specific and simple as possible. For example: "I would like to have a peaceful day with my office-mates," or "I would like to get the tire on my bike fixed."

5. Each person says "ready" when they have their request for the day in mind.
   (Keep a record book. One person serves as the recorder, writing the date, each person's name, their request or concern, and leaving space after each name for the answer that results from the meditation. An example of this will follow the directions.)

6. Close your eyes again and ask the universe, God, your inner teacher, your larger mind, your less conscious awareness (or whatever image you feel comfortable with) for help with your concern for the day.

7. One person leads a guided image that:
   a. takes you someplace, and
   b. stops at an object or person that will give you your answer. Example: Go to a stream . . . a fish comes to the surface and gives you your answer. (See other examples at the end of this section.)

8. Each person says "ready" when they have their answers.

9. The recorder writes down the answer under the concern and lets the person have time to tell about how the answer came, if they choose. (Example:

The fish was a shark and the answer was written on its teeth.)

10. Join hands, sing, say a familiar verse, send love, or just sit quietly.

11. Follow the guidance that was suggested for the day. (Most important!)

12. Release what has transpired here. Don't have a meeting later to see if you have accomplished your goals. That is not the channel we are playing with here. Let it go without judgment. The notes are a record for anyone who really wants to tally effectiveness. (If people start asking for results, then the emphasis will be on achieving or cheating and will be completely off the process of listening to another level of consciousness. This process doesn't need the same glare of judgment we shine on other parts of our day and life.)

13. If, after you get used to it, this process takes more than ten minutes for four people, then you may be making it too long and stretching some people's patience. If you don't want to lose them or invalidate the process, I suggest that you keep it as short as possible when using it as an opening to a meeting or as part of another activity. Keep it *short* and *make* time for it.

Note that a group process does not need to be called "meditation" if you feel that the word would stop some people from participating. Call it "a moment of reflection to seek guidance from our larger minds." Call it "the start of the meeting." Call it "something the boss says we have to do." Call it any acceptable label or give it none at all; simply allow it to bring the group closer together. This process can be used in any group with a strong leader who believes enough in the process to put it high on the priority list.

Some examples from our family record:

SUE: I'd like help with always feeling I'm rushing.

ANS: Take deep breaths throughout the day . . . see all the little wonders . . . be full of curiosity like a kid.

AMY: I'd like help with my feelings.

ANS: Whenever you feel mad just ask God for help.

JED: I need help getting ready for our trip with ease and comfort.

ANS: Run in the morning, enjoy the preparation, and don't worry about the future.

AARON: I'd like help getting back on schedule for baseball.

ANS: Eat better breakfasts.

CARLIN: I would like help keeping the spiritual focus and expansion I felt last night.

ANS: Make plans for the retreat, meditate, and breathe.

AMY: I need help with a peaceful day.

ANS: Send out lots of love to family and friends.

One further suggestion: Change as little as possible the way children word their concerns and answers. First trust that they know what they are asking for and hearing, then, if it seems really unintelligible, ask the child to state it again so it makes sense to you.

Here are some suggestions for guided images to get you started. They are stated very simply. You may elaborate as you desire but watch out for getting so distracted with the image that you lose the point of the journey.

- Walk along a downtown street, enter a store, and something in that store will have an answer for you.
- Get on an airplane . . . the flight attendant has your answer.
- Walk in the country . . . an animal comes up to you with the answer.
- Go to the library . . . a book on the shelf falls on you and the answer is the title.

- The phone rings . . . the person on the other end gives you the answer.
- Write out your request for the day . . . the answer is on the pen you are using.
- Go to a Chinese restaurant . . . the answer is in the fortune cookie.
- A beautiful plant grows before your eyes . . . it blooms and your answer is in the blossom.
- A car drives by on the freeway . . . the answer is on its license plate.
- Get on a bus . . . the answer is on one of the seats.
- Take a trip to outer space . . . the galaxy you visit has a planet in it with your answer.

When I have taught this technique at workshops, people often get so carried away with the image that they forget about the message they went after. This may be a reflection of the way we conduct our lives. Our minds are quick and wonderfully responsive, so we can let the answers come quickly. They will if we expect them to. We won't always take the time to gather our incense and meditation blanket, take off our shoes, assume a certain posture, light a candle, and breathe deeply for twenty minutes—all before consulting our inner voice. We all can and will, with a little practice, be enticed to stop for sixty seconds to state our problem and open an imaginary fortune cookie for an answer.

I started this process for myself in the bathroom of a school where I was teaching. This was the only place where my privacy was respected for sixty seconds. It was my sanctuary, my place to collect myself and check in for guidance from my other levels of awareness in peace and quiet. Examine your environment and take what is available for you. That bathroom served me well.

Children have taught me a great deal about responding quickly. Their minds work rapidly, being very straightforward. When I ask them to relax they do it *right now*. They haven't yet been programmed by adults to believe they can't just relax at will. The same instant response can go for problems and answers. They move into the fantasy easily, open the cookie, and take delight in the answer. Appeal to the child in you to return with spontaneity, delight, and presence in the moment. Be your child and approach the meditation with a "Wow!" See with new eyes and feel the excitement of the adventure ahead.

This group process, like the individual meditation suggestions in Chapters Six and Seven, will work to the degree that you prioritize it in your group. Problems may arise; for example, in our family group we have had to deal with people who thought that the process was too long. We have also encountered someone who was always late, and we addressed that and moved through it as well. Stay with the practice as consistently as you would the need to brush your teeth.

Often, when a person is new to the practice, they may have trouble getting an answer, or it may take a long time. Most likely this is because their mind is wandering. As the mind wanders it not only gets off track, but it spends its time thinking of reasons that the answers can't work or dreaming up infinite options. At this point the person may well be so confused that they don't know what the real answer is. (This is a reason for encouraging acceptance of immediate, first answers.) One answer to this problem is to suggest to the person that they accept any answer at this point, even if it seems illogical, unfitting, or even silly. Often we censor the answer as something we don't want to do, or something too expensive or time consuming, or something someone else will think us foolish to be doing, and so on. We are not properly respectful of how fast our censor works! The mind can reject an idea before you can conceive even a single thought about it. It is as if a fencer parried before he even thrust. We stop ourselves before we start.

A clear example of this came to my attention in our family group one day. Ten-year-old Aaron usually gets his images and answers faster than any of us, but this time he suddenly began to lag behind. I noticed from his restless body movements that his concentration was wandering. He seemed to be patiently waiting for something. I finally asked him why he had slowed down and he said, "Amy is always last, she always waits until after me."

Aha!—sibling competition in reverse. I suggested that his attention on that detail was taking his attention off the process. Aaron was getting distracted from the process by getting into a game with his sister; therefore, he was not getting his answers. I told him if he would do what was right for him Amy would also drop her part in the game. He was heard and it seemed to drop away easily.

Another story that was fun for us all is about Jed's teenage son Jason, who spends part of each summer with us. We really wanted him to share in our family morning activity, but 7:30 AM to a teenager on vacation seemed to be an impossible hurdle. We appealed to his big brother energy by telling him how we felt the process had helped Amy in her relationships. We explained that his example could help reinforce the process for her. He agreed to participate one day of each week. In meditation he asked for some good skateboarding connections and within a few days he found two half-pipes (tracks to skateboard on) and a couple of nice friends. That was enough to sell him on the process and ensure his continued participation, and this was a delight to us all.

The process is similar to getting someone to go with you to a flea market for the first time. The group meditation, like the flea market, may seem confusing at first, but once you focus and find your first treasure or bargain, you are sold, and you have a new tool that is yours to keep.

The value of group meditation can be found in the most practical realms. With his own money, Aaron had purchased a toy, only to find he couldn't make it work. The next morning he asked for help in learning to use the toy. He heard how to make the toy work in specific detail and dashed from the meeting to try it out. It worked! He was thrilled and excited. As a little aside here: the night before I felt parental guilt for not dashing to his rescue, reinforcing his trust in my abilities, and saving him from this trauma. I had a deadline to meet and didn't want to take the time to help him. This allowed him to solve his own problem the following morning and also to put some of his trust in resources other than Mom. I mention this to encourage you to build your confidence in following your feelings. Your part of the interaction is as right for you as it is for the other person. We recognize this at some step along the way if we are patient and trust enough.

I felt that all of our interest was lagging at one point, and it was especially noticeable in Amy. I knew that I was quite invested in having her do the meditations because I believed they could help shift her to believe in her own power and resourcefulness, but she was barely going through the motions. I meditated and concluded that Amy, Aaron, and I doing this process without Jed would not work. (We have family agreements about who does what activity, attempting to equalize our parental involvements. Sometimes a division of labor made according to logic doesn't make sense on a larger level.)

Jed was doing evening stories and felt reluctance to extend himself further, but he meditated and decided that it was the right time for him to join the morning stories and meditation. Jed started coming and Amy, after a proper interval of protest, started participating more fully. Our family harmony took a giant step forward. Taking Amy and Aaron to our family retreats and having them teach others the process was a bonus to all, a delight for us, and reinforcement for them both.

A child may protest joining in such an activity, yet feel left out if they are not participating. If we as parents understand the importance of this process for maintaining family unity, we will raise this activity to top priority. (Do you recall the tooth brushing versus meditation analogy in Chapter Six?) As we adults set the example, the children, each in his or her individual way, responded and our family communications improved greatly.

Four years later we are still doing our morning meditations. Although I will not say they are a cure-all, I will say that they help keep us all in touch on a level of consciousness that is not easily explained. We are a busy family, always going our separate ways, and these family meditations are an important anchor for us.

MEETINGS THAT HEAL SEPARATION AND PROMOTE JOINING

Our family meetings occur once a week. They provide a place where we can each be heard equally and a place where we can ask for help from other family members. This format can be used for any group that desires more cooperation among its members.

1. One person reads the minutes from the last meeting checking to see if all commitments have been met. If not, they are recorded again as part of the current minutes. Each member takes a turn recording minutes and leading the meeting. The name of each person in attendance is noted.

2. Start with a song, verse, holding hands, or anything that feels like a joining gesture.

3. Early in the meeting do *one* of the following (no one is *required* to participate):

   a. Compliments and Brags: Compliment another group member for help received from them or for some action that you noticed during the week. A brag is about anything you feel proud to have accomplished during the week.

   b. Each person has the opportunity to state something they are appreciative of about themselves or others in the group.

   c. Each person has the opportunity to share what they are thankful for.

4. Confidentiality within the group must be respected.

5. Announcements important to individual members are shared and calendar dates verified. Family activities can be planned and dates set.

6. This can be a time to ask for something personal. Perhaps one person would like help from someone else, the group in general, or a volunteer. This is the time to ask for help—the request is recorded in the minutes as a gentle reminder, and a date is set to accomplish the task. This step can be empowering for quieter members of the group.

7. A time to ask for help with group responsibilities. Perhaps the maintenance of the house, office, shop, meeting room, newsletter, or whatever is in need of some revision. The concern is stated, suggestions for improvement are heard, volunteers are found to help, commitments are recorded, and dates (if applicable) are set.

8. Sharing personal troubles or joys. I may just want a safe place to talk, or I may want to share something that has been weighing on my mind. I don't necessarily want advice; I just want to be heard by people I care about. My behavior will be affecting these people if I have a weighty problem. Sometimes just sharing that I have this problem is enough, without going into detail. And I may ask for advice, or another viewpoint on my situation, if I want. There are many uses for this space.

9. A time to share things that "bug" or annoy us. No feedback is allowed here. We simply listen.

10. Set goals for yourself or for the group that can be accomplished in a certain time period. We commit to both short-range and long-range goals in our group.

11. Set the next meeting time. It is best to have a regular time. Select a leader and scribe for next time.

12. Finish with a closing touch, song, verse, saying, silence, hand-holding, massage, or anything that

promotes warmth and unity before breaking up. Each person doing whatever they want to during the silence can also be a powerful joining.

Keep the meetings in the thirty-to-sixty-minute range, if possible. All of the above suggestions are ideas to be spread out over many meetings as you grow accustomed to one another and determine the methods most suitable for your particular group. Especially in families with small children, keep things moving and brief, so that the little ones will be able to last throughout the session. This will help them to feel like a necessary and wanted part of the group.

Be vigilant in not allowing your meetings to slip into an adult business meeting to "shape up" the family. Children will let this happen out of fear of going against adult wishes. You will know if the meetings are meeting the childrens' needs by their interest level. Our children ask regularly for "Compliments and Brags" and "Bugs"—a sign of their genuine interest in the process. I suggest that when you are new to these meetings, and your children are participating, focus the meetings on these two activities and concentrate less on family planning at first. In past family meetings, we have enjoyed planning an "unbirthday" party, a family trip to a hot springs, various children's activities, and overnight trips to relatives.

Use your wonderfully creative imaginations to develop other ways of enriching your group experiences. This is a time to equalize the power structure in the group, *not* a time to reinforce authority channels with added group pressure. Use the suggested structure as a skeleton on which to hang your own brand of creative responses that can increase your group's spontaneous communication in a safe atmosphere.

One of the greatest benefits from this process is that no one has to be in the role of the group scold. The following two examples illustrate how this works:

Jed offered to fix Aaron's bike. A few weeks rolled by and each time it was read in the minutes Jed would say, "Oh, no!" Aaron would good-naturedly watch him squirm at being reminded of his promise. Each time, Aaron felt heard and empowered by the process. Jed had to recommit each week until the task was accomplished.

An *equal* power group is really important in parent/ boss/authority vs. child/employee/less-powerful relationships. If the balance of power is not maintained, the resulting disparity is harder to reconcile than in a more equal relationship. In families it is so easy to forget a child's needs. Parents often teach children to scream and demand before being heard. A group where all can be heard and supported is a powerful vehicle for teaching children to express themselves honestly.

Another time, Amy owed Sue $3.50. This was read in the minutes without comment for three months. There was no verbal comment, but plenty of heavy energy circulated through the whole group every time it was read. Some comments started creeping in: "Did you borrow this money or did she give it to you?" and "Do you plan to pay her back?" Finally I said I was tired of hearing about this debt and wanted some resolution with a date put on it, now. Amy reluctantly made a commitment and Jed offered to help her keep it. I use this as an example of how easily something can be lost in the shuffle of family busy-ness. Without the family meeting I suspect that Amy would have outwaited Sue's patience. Sue would have thought "forget it," and would have dropped it with nothing more said. However, the memories and feelings would remain and the separation between them would have continued. Amy would have gotten away with something on the surface but would also, on some level, have been carrying around the guilt. This was bound to result in some manifestation in her behavior, eventually.

Group meditation is a rough jewel awaiting that special brand of polish from your group. It is a powerful tool that reaches beyond simple improvement of surface behavior to go deep into our psyche with helpful and loving encouragement. I know this process is worth it when I see a child with quivering chin say something about their feelings that I suspect they would have otherwise buried until such time as they might reveal it to a sensitive listener, if they are lucky enough to encounter such a person later in their life. Groups can provide a place where everyone can feel they are being heard. The time spent in this process will pay long-range dividends that are difficult to measure . . . only at the start.

Epilogue

In writing this book, I hope to accomplish the following goals:

- To bring you nourishment and encouragement for your individual spiritual path. And to assure you that you are all right and are already intuitively doing what is right for you in your life at this time.

- To remind you that the energy you send out is what you receive back. Giving is *truly* an act of instant receiving.

- To help you to see that the form doesn't matter nearly as much as the process. In the larger picture, "what" you are doing doesn't mean as much as "how" you are doing it.

- To suggest that you are creating your reality every second of your life. You are not stuck. There is no "right" way to fashion your life.

You do have choices and you can choose again at any time. Being a victim is a choice and you can just as easily choose another way.

- To consider that pain can be your friend and teacher, and it can guide you out of your dark places. And that the greatest pain is when we separate ourselves from others with judgments, labeling, comparisons, and so forth. Being free of divisive ways of thinking is true freedom.

- To encourage you to choose peace of mind and love over confusion and fear. Joining as opposed to separating is the true place of harmony and peace of mind.

- To assure you that you can start new habits in your life now which, with practice, will override the old ones you have outgrown.

There are three stages in the process of spiritual evolution:

1. Mind—clearly getting the concepts that will be helpful to you in your mind. This is easy. Millions have listened to speakers and have read thousands of books and can quote you all of the right words and emotion-stirring phrases.

2. Action—put some of the concepts into your deliberate actions. This includes using some of the practices suggested in this book and establishing a program to change some of your habitual behavior so that it serves you and your present consciousness. Now is the time for *patience* with yourself and continued *persistance* and *perseverance.*

3. Automatize—watch to see when your new behavior becomes an automatic response. This is when your program of maintenance is regular and you immediately think of which practice to turn to when you feel constricted and heavy with burdens. This is when you attend to a situation with peace of mind.

You do it smoothly and with such clarity that you don't even notice the beauty of the moment at times. It is later, maybe even days later, that you think back on how wonderful it feels to have acted from such a deep and peaceful place in your being. To have the thoughts and actions that you want in life coming from your automatic and habitual reactions is pure joy. How fulfilling and beautiful it feels to automatically do the most loving and helpful thing in the moment without even thinking about it! It can all be yours simply by making a commitment to go deeper within your own being for your spiritual nourishment.

This book can be used as a foundation; it describes certain knowledge that is essential for communication and participation in the process of spiritual evolution. This book has been designed to help you see more clearly and let go of a lot of your early conditioning and the mind clutter which is not serving you well at this time. If you are always busy, preoccupied, angry, fearful, fixing up "wrongs," and dealing with the emergencies you have created, how can you possibly expect yourself to be available for spiritual growth? You are weighed down. Your vision is clouded. Your senses are dulled. Let this book help you to shed these weights, lift the veils, quiet the sounds, so you can breathe and see and listen to something broader and deeper in your life experience which is trying so lovingly to get your attention.

With the practices outlined in this book you can set aside a lifetime of conditioning and open to a fresh way of addressing your world. In this process of lightening your burdens, your senses will open to sights, sounds, feelings, intuitions, and perceptions—all are your birthright, waiting to be claimed.

Most of us have been denying ourselves our full awareness by keeping our perceptions confined to a tiny, measurable reality. This "reality" is kept in control by what we *think* we know. We are afraid to add more data to our long-held belief systems for fear of change or of being "wrong."

My fondest wish for my book, for you, and for the world would be fulfilled if you have felt a gentle trusting smile of understanding somewhere deep inside of you as you read through these pages. This little touch of joining can help you to feel so beautifully content with this moment in life. Participating and appreciating in this moment . . . right now . . . asking for no more, is true contentment.

If I could give you one gift to go with you always, it would be peace of mind. I will do the closest thing I know how. I promise to maintain peace of mind in my being, knowing that this is my gift of joining with our whole world and that my peace of mind reflects out into an equally peaceful world.

Peace of mind is not a passive state. It is a feeling of being right just as you are and of being in the right place at the right time. It is the comfort of knowing deep within that your puzzle piece fits and the whole puzzle needs your piece to be complete. Peace of mind can be saying "no" or "yes," or not saying anything at all. It is not the process, but the feeling of harmony and of joining during and after the commission of the process.

I have deliberately omitted a list of reference books at the end. When we don't understand or feel uncomfortable with something, often our tendency is to look to other sources, hoping that one of them will say it just right to *make* something happen to us. Then we give credit to the person or book that was with us when we made this breakthrough. This is simply more of the subtle separation and victim stance in action; it is *not* how the process works. No one can make it happen for you until you are ready to accept full responsibility for your life. Then everything and everyone is your teacher. This book is about letting go of waiting for the special magic fairy who will come someday to "fix us up." It is about taking personal responsibility for being your fullest and highest self, now.

When you are ready to make a commitment to explore your fullest spiritual potentiality, this book will guide you.

Or, if you prefer, go to another book but then go no further. Stop with one book, one person, one relationship, one philosophy, one idea, one sea shell, and *be with it.* Then stay with what you have chosen, *ask* for what you want, *meditate,* and you will *find* what you are seeking.

All you need is within you and you can hear the guidance through your own meditation process.

And now let us begin with this moment.

When the clarity
of who I really am
communes with
the order of the universe—
My deepest recesses
Sing in harmony
and
My relationships
Reflect confirmation
of purity and completeness

About the Author

I am a counselor, teacher, astrologer, yoga instructor, musician, healer, mother, wife, and student of the universe. My teaching experience, from elementary through college levels, spans twenty-five years. My business card succinctly sums up the whole: "Free-lance Spirituality Consultant."

I conduct workshops, seminars, and retreats and take individuals for extended spiritual study and practice. We come together to celebrate the sacred in each other, and together we nurture the most vulnerable, tender, and sensitive parts of our inner being. We help each other to throw off layers of defensiveness, armor, and separation disguised as cynicism, anger, and despair. We cultivate new habits that serve our present circumstances and nourish the sturdy seed of our unconditional love. We have ceremonies to celebrate our modern-day Rite of Passage and continue to be a support network after the rush of new-found awareness wanes and continued maintenance of practices is desired. We help each other with new habits we want to sustain in our newly established prospering relationship with life. As we maintain peace of mind for ourselves, it is also our powerful and ever present gift to our world.

There is no more to *say*, it is time to *do*. I am sitting in the quiet of my "playroom" (called by some an office) wishing for you the peace of mind and the enthusiasm for life that I feel at this moment.

My husband has a special interest in working with men and has done therapy and led groups for the past twenty years. Jed and I facilitate workshops and seminars through the Center for Prospering Relationships that are related to "Men's Issues." These activities are for men and women who want to explore the issues of masculinity and femininity as they affect us in our culture, the choices we have within the gender we have chosen, and the broader spiritual scope of what male and female are to each of us historically and in the present.

I invite you to write me:

Carlin J. Diamond
Center for Prospering Relationships
Post Office Box 9355
San Rafael, CA 94912
(415) 472-4649

With joy and love to you,

Carlin

One step in learning to let go of labeling was to let go of prejudging with my eyes. This came home to me once as I was in the process of being selected for a jury. I watched the two male defendants, sporting fresh haircuts and new suits, who sat awaiting their trial. I wondered if that's how they looked when they were arrested and how much their present looks would affect my judgment of their innocence or guilt.

I have seen clothing as costume since I was a teenager. "Costuming" myself seemed a most appropriate way to make a visual statement supporting the title of this book. I have yet to make the childhood cliche, "Don't judge a book by its cover," into a complete reality in my life. I feel that its message could penetrate deeper into all of our consciousness if we would address it.

I have entertained fantasies of being the person in each of these poses and feel a fragment of each one is also a part of me. Themes from my book ran through my mind as I watched people's reactions and listened to their comments as I paraded the streets being photographed in my various guises.

We all have richly varied and many-faceted personalities awaiting discovery. What we praise or condemn in others is simply something awaiting recognition and expression in ourselves. When we learn to *love it* rather than *label it*, we are on our way to fully appreciating our less conscious levels of awareness.

To All And Everyone
Lest
I Contribute
To The Separation
I Ask You To Examine
In This Book

My sincere gratitude to all who have helped with the production of this book. I honor you all, the babies to the old ones, from spirits to rocks and from colors to thoughts with gratitude and appreciation as limitless as space. To distinguish for a list of acknowledgments is counter to the joining I am hoping to encourage by writing this book. To separate for giving credit perpetuates the thesis of this book that separation by labeling results in most of the pain that we experience in life. Let us join in celebrating the birth of this book and in appreciating equally all who have nurtured and influenced the author. I embrace you all and trust that you know that your seeds are planted in this garden.

LIFE READING
with
CARLIN DIAMOND
Free Lance Spirituality Consultant

Reading Includes:
- Personal Astrological Update
- Relevant Past Lives
- Spiritual/Mystical Purpose
- Support with Present Situations, Life Course Decisions, and Relationships
- Visualizations for Healing

Center for Prospering Relationships
P.O. Box 9355, San Rafael, CA 94912
(415) 472-4649

ORDER FORM

Fifth Wave Press
P.O. Box 9355
San Rafael, CA 94912
(415) 472-4649

Send Check or Money Order to Fifth Wave Press.
Shipping is $1.50 for 1st item and $.50 for each
additional item up to $5.00 maximum. California
residents add 6% sales tax. Additional discounts
for larger quantities, check for information below.

Qty.	Title	Price	Amount
_____	LOVE IT, DON'T LABEL IT	$10.00	_____
	TAPES		
_____	Selections from the book and Songs by Author & Chris Thomerson	$10.00	_____
_____	Meditation	$10.00	_____
_____	Meditation for Children	$10.00	_____
_____	Yoga with Carlin	$10.00	_____

	Subtotal	_____
	Sales Tax	_____
	Shipping Total	_____

Name_____

Address_____

City_____State_____Zip_____

Phone_____

INFORMATION FORM

I would like more information on the following:
_____ Sponsoring a seminar/workshop in my area
_____ Hosting a book party in my area
_____ Committed Spiritual Study
_____ Private Consultations
_____ Astrological Counseling
_____ Yoga Instruction
_____ Schedule of Seminars and Workshops